Plan
Your Own Landscape

Plan
Your Own Landscape

by
Allan A. Swenson

Designs by Peter J. Swenson
Illustrations by Jeff Fallon

Publishers · GROSSET & DUNLAP · New York
A FILMWAYS COMPANY

712

To Peter Jon Swenson, with gratitude for your untiring efforts to help plan this book as you planned and planted beautiful plantscapes. May your own landscaping future grow, bloom, and be most abundant and rewarding.

Photographs on pages viii, 4, 20, and 22 courtesy of the O. M. Scott & Sons Company.

Contents

Acknowledgments

Grateful thanks are due to all who advised and guided me in the preparation of this practical guide to planning, planting, and maintaining a lovelier landscape for homes across America. Special thanks are due Wayne Cutting for his creative landscapemanship, Robert Palmer for his thoughtful advice, Ray Bergeron for his common sense and down-to-earth guidance, and the many others at landscape firms, horticultural colleges, and the many sound basic home gardeners as well. Your help was most welcome and appreciated.

Introduction

You can make your own portion of the planet Earth lovelier. You can plan and plant trees and shrubs, hedges and flowers, build beds and borders that bloom and bear beautifully. It's easier than you think to grow and groom your own home grounds.

The first step is thoughtful planning. It isn't necessary to be a landscape architect either, although they're mighty helpful for professional advice on major projects. However, more families and individuals are becoming aware of the value of attractive landscaping, not only to their own sense of beauty and improvement of their home environment, but to increase the real estate value of their property as well.

There's an important move afoot to beautify America. Flower seed and plant sales are climbing. Nurseries report increased sales of trees and shrubs. Real estate brokers point out that home values can increase from $1,500 to $3,000 because of better landscaping.

You can do most of the planning and planting yourself. In older homes you can renovate, prune, and revitalize. It's fun, it's easier than you imagine, and it's rewarding. This book is designed to guide you step by step. Experts in design, landscaping, planting, and care of gardens have helped develop these down-to-earth basics and the more advanced planning and landscaping ideas and methods.

You'll find typical plans and blueprints and actual graphs and plant-design outlines from which to lay out your own home landscapes. You'll also find lists of shrubs and trees that perform well and thrive in various parts of the country.

There are good guides, too, for tastier living from fruitful landscaping. You'll learn how to use decorative accents and specimens to create visually appealing home plantscapes.

Most important, of course, is the basic plan. From this book, you can plot out your growing landscape success. You'll find samples of typical landscape plans for a ranch house, a colonial style, or an older home, as well as ways to solve difficult areas like slopes and shady areas.

Included are guides you can use to trace your own plan and to position trees, shrubs, hedges, patios, and gardens, as you blueprint your lovelier living landscape.

A beautiful home is a treat and a joy. Just as important as adding beauty, you add dollar value to your home with an attractive landscape. It makes sense and it makes dollars, too. This book is designed to provide all the basic information and ground rules so you can plan and plant your own lovelier landscape.

Trees and shrubs provide peaceful, attractive privacy areas for lovelier outdoor living.

1.

Landscaping Your Growing Investment

Attractive, well planned and planted landscaping is an investment that grows for you. Not only do you enjoy the beauty of trees and shrubs, flowers and fruit, sweeping expanses of lush lawns, but your property becomes a more enjoyable outdoor environment for friends and neighbors too. Just as important, a well planted and maintained home ground adds real dollar value to your home.

Fact is, research projects by the Forest Service, colleges, private groups and firms have established some amazing facts. A well landscaped home will sell for as much as 20 percent more than a similar house without trees, shrubs, plants and a healthy lawn. Not only will a house sell for more, it will sell faster and easier. One survey of about 200 interviews revealed that a home with an abundance of trees had a much greater sales appeal than one without.

Surveys of real estate agents around America also emphasized the importance and real value of landscaping. An attractive lawn around a medium-priced home added an average of $1322 to its resale value. Another more recent survey compiled data on a variety of homes. It demonstrated that a well kept lawn increased home values an average of $1421.

When trees, shrubs and other plantings were added and compared with homes not so neatly landscaped or well designed in their landscape balance, effective landscaping added more than $1800 on average compared to homes with poor landscaping, but similar in style, number of rooms and other basic considerations.

Real estate brokers pointed out another interesting fact as they stressed the value of attention to landscaping. The condition of the gardens is an important factor in influencing home buyers. Well maintained, healthy trees, shrubs and flowers add to the price and the speed of sale, they pointed out, because buyers believe the house too will be as well kept as the landscape.

Other reports confirmed the facts in different ways. There is no doubt that the extra time and effort put into planning a lovelier landscape which sets your home

Attractive, inviting, well-maintained lawns and home landscapes add beauty and real dollar value to your home.

off to the most appealing, natural way, is well worthwhile. That's dollar value added on to the pleasure you gain from gardening and enjoying the beauty that surrounds you in an attractively designed plantscape. For many, that is reward enough. It is nice to know, however, that one's efforts are rewarded in more ways than one, especially when it comes time to sell your home.

In addition, nurserymen, college researchers, private landscape firms and others point out many other values of landscaping. As you consider upgrading your property, revitalizing older overgrown plantings or improving on what you already have begun, perhaps in your first home, here is food for thought.

Landscaping will help you get maximum use from your home grounds. By planting for play areas, work areas, vegetable and fruit gardens, you can put your grounds to greater productivity and fun.

Proper landscape design also means easier maintenance. If you avoid a jumble of trees and shrubs, care is easier and takes less time. If you plan for flow of people well, you'll save thousands of steps a year in garden chores and just plain here and there walking.

You also can achieve greater privacy in our hectic, hustling world. Noisy neighbors can be screened out with hedges and other plantings. Nearby unsightly views of street, stores, traffic can be buffered by trees and shrubs.

Cities have cleaned up their air somewhat. Trees and green living plants not only reduce noise, but they also trap soot and dirt as they act as filters for the air we breathe. Rains wash these residues off leaves back to the ground.

Highway departments have revealed that hedgerow planting of dense shrubs and parallel lines of trees can reduce noise pollution by many decibels. It is much quieter on your private side of hedges and tree belts. That's quiet good news.

In this energy-conscious world, landscaping also can help conserve energy. Well planned landscape elements can reduce home heating and cooling both, by 25 percent or more. Not all can have this saving, true. But trees, living fences and shrubs reduce the wind-chill factor that hits homes, forcing heat losses. In Midwestern farm areas, windbreaks of trees have long been aids to keeping warm in winter and saving fuel.

Trees are nature's air conditioners. They do much more than merely provide a visually pleasant environment. By providing shade during summer months, they add an element of climate control.

Surface temperature of roofs and walls is reduced by 8 to 15 degrees when shaded by trees. That saves electricity on air conditioning.

Trees also transpire tremendous amounts of water daily. This is the heart of many cooling systems. You can even plant trees to funnel breezes to certain parts of your home grounds. By choosing deciduous trees that lose their leaves in winter, the sun will shine through bare branches to provide warming value on your home. Evergreens planted as a windbreak may cut fuel bills substantially.

Recent studies indicate that properly planted and positioned trees along a busy street can reduce noise penetrating to surrounding areas by as much as 60 percent. That saves your ears. The trees also screen out traffic visually to provide greater privacy if you live near busy roads and highways.

Shrubs do their part too in a balanced landscape. They also take in carbon dioxide and give off oxygen in their life process. That's a fair exchange. Fact is, without

Shrubs and trees lend natural beauty to your home entrance.

foliage, animals and man would be in serious trouble.

Continuing research on the value of trees and shrubs recently has revealed other benefits in quantitative terms. Experiments in the Midwest reveal shelterbelts are actually more valuable than people realized in fuel conservation. In one experiment, fuel consumption was 25 percent less in a house protected on the windward side by a shelterbelt than in an identical but unprotected home. When the house was sheltered on three sides, but open on the southern side, there was a 70 percent reduction in wind and 40 percent savings in fuel. That's welcome news as home heating costs climb.

Other tests revealed that a solid barrier of evergreens is not the ideal solution. It creates excessive turbulence on the side away from the wind which accentuates heat loss from the supposedly protected building. A barrier of trees that allows some air passage and prevents turbulence is more effective.

Most winds come from northern or northwesterly directions. A windbreak on north and westerly sides with some on the eastern usually works best.

Consider your landscape trees as natural air conditioning allies in warmer climates when you plan your landscaping. Here are some revealing findings. Shade trees helped reduce air conditioning costs by almost half compared to un-shaded homes in sunny climates. Another finding showed that shaded outside walls were 5 to 10 degrees cooler than unshaded walls.

Today, these findings are more important than ever. Not only can you save heating costs, cut air conditioning expenses and enjoy the beauty of trees, but lovelier living landscapes are like money in the bank, if and when you sell your home.

As you plan your own landscape, plan first for the appearance and look you like. Add in those windbreak and shading factors too. Your total plan can be richly rewarding in appearance as well as a growing investment year by year.

Trees, shrubs, and flowers blend with a manicured lawn to provide a perfect panorama of beauty for your home grounds.

2.

Soil, Site, and Growing Needs

Beautiful landscapes begin in the good earth. Your plants must have a fertile footing in which they can establish a firm, steady, happy roothold for years of good growing.

You may already have suitable soil where you live. You may also have backfill around your home's foundation from hasty cover-up by a contractor. You may find sand or clay soil. Don't fret. With a little extra effort, even poor soils can be improved to support successful landscape plant growth.

Sandy soil won't hold moisture well; plants can dry out. Clay soil holds too much water; plant roots can rot. Debris in the ground can give shrubs and trees rooting fits. No matter what you find as you dig in, you can change and improve the growing conditions. It's easier than you imagine.

Soil is alive. It is being formed constantly from the decomposition of organic matter together with the breakdown of rock and mineral in the subsoil. With additives, you can build its fertility well. The key to soil improvement is working with nature. Look over your home grounds. Plants need sun to manufacture their food. The roots extract nutrients from soil and these nutrients, dissolved in water, are absorbed and moved into leaf areas. There, with chlorophyll as a catalyst, they convert the sun's energy into plant foods. You may have shady areas as well as full sun locations. Consider plant compatability.

Some plants prefer shade. You can actually make shady spots sparkle with flowering shrubs and plants that like shade. Others prefer moist growing conditions *and* shade. Many prefer lots of sun. Some like drier soil. In this book you can find lists of a wide range of plants and their needs for sun or shade, moist or dry conditions. It pays to place plants in the conditions they prefer, so they will thrive and perform to the best potential.

Avoid wet areas if possible. You can use these as wild gardens, natural settings, even bog-garden plantings. Or you can install underground tile drains—which unfortunately are expensive.

6

You cannot, of course, alter the sun. You can remove a building or cut down old trees in poor condition to open areas to sunlight. Some plants won't thrive in harsh winters or when exposed to chilling, drying winds. In this book, you will also find a horticulture zone map and table of indicator plants. These are designed as guides to those trees and shrubs that will prosper in various climatic zones and survive winters there. You will also find guides to a wide selection of flowers as well as shrubs, with tips about their hardiness and growing preferences. Other source books on plants and their needs cover the tens of thousands of different types available to you.

As you plan your lovelier landscaping, comparing plants and selecting those you want, remember that their health and happiness begins in the good earth. Here's how to improve the soil from the ground up.

Soil is truly alive. Millions of microorganisms are at work in it, breaking down minerals and organic matter. You can help them produce better soil. Compost, leaf mold, peat moss, and other types of organic matter are important for soil. Indeed, no soil can have too much organic matter. As you improve the structure of soil by adding organic matter, you open up the soil so it can pick up more nutrients. Fertilizer can work more effectively in porous, friable soil where roots can pick it up and use it to build more leaves, stems, and trunks, as well as flowers and fruits.

Soil improvement involves a balance in structure, texture, and porosity. When you pick up a handful of rich soil, it should crumble easily in your hands. There are, of course, unseen factors affecting the soil, such as the nutrient level. But you can add nutrients later, and as necessary each year. Your first step should be rebuilding the soil to a granular feel with clusters that readily shake apart. You can buy loam by the load. That's expensive and usually needless, unless you have exceedingly poor soil and backfill around your home.

When you have selected the planting sites, dig in. Remove rocks and debris. If soil is sandy or clayey, use this mixture to improve it: Combine equal parts of peat moss, and composted humus with the topsoil. Turn with a fork or spade. If you prefer, spread peat and composted humus on the surface and rototill it under.

Peat moss and humus mainly improve soil structure. If soil is sandy, the peat and humus help it retain moisture longer so plant roots can obtain that needed moisture. If soil has high clay content and remains wet too long, peat and compost will open up the soil to improve draining. Plant roots must breathe. Excess water in soil also rots roots. Improving soil structure helps solve these problems. It may require several years to build a really good soil condition, but your long-range results will be well worth the extra effort.

Compost is a key. You can buy composted humus in bags and peat moss in bales. You also can easily make composted humus. A compost pile is nothing more exotic than a cinderblock, wire, or other structure in which you pile organic material. This can include grass clippings, leaves of vegetables, or tree leaves you rake each fall. You can add old straw and mulch, peat moss—just about any type of vegetation that will rot down.

Two types of soil bacteria digest organic material. If you turn the compost pile every day or so by spading fork, the aerobic bacteria are encouraged to work more quickly. They need air to do their digestive duties on old plant material. You can achieve well-decomposed compost to improve soil within a month. Moisten the pile each week to speed decomposition.

A slower method utilizes the anaerobic bacteria. Just pile organic materials in a corner. Leave a slight depression on top to collect rain. Sprinkle the pile periodically in dry times. Within several months, this material will rot down into rich, dark, valuable, soil-improving humus.

Worms also speed up decomposition. You may also add a few cupfuls of fertilizer or a layer of manure several inches thick. This adds nutrients to the small quantities present in the organic matter itself.

You can improve soil right in place, too. Use mulch continuously. Mulch is any organic material, such as grass clippings, old spoiled farm hay, old leaves from trees, peat moss, or wood chips, that does triple duty. It smothers weeds and helps prevent weed seeds from sprouting. It also helps soil retain moisture where plant roots can utilize it. Third, organic mulches rot down slowly to improve soil condition and add minor amounts of nutrients to soil. You can turn these materials under periodically to speed up soil improvement, or just let them do their work more slowly in place on the soil surface.

If you use wood and bark chips, they don't decompose too well. When they do, they may create acid conditions, especially pine bark or pine needles. They may also, in the decomposition process, utilize nitrogen from the soil that plants need. You can compensate easily for this by adding a balanced commercial fertilizer to the surface and scratching it in with a rake before adding water to help dissolve it. To counteract acid conditions, you can add lime and water it into the mulch later. Remember, however, that some plants, like azaleas, rhododendrons, and their relatives, prefer more acid soil conditions to thrive.

When you prepare planting sites for flower beds and borders, shrubs and other plants, you can improve soil just in those specific locations. That saves the work of doing complete areas at one time. Here's how:

Dig the hole for the plant or shrub larger and deeper than the root ball actually requires. Remove poor subsoil, rocks, and debris. Then mix equal parts of compost and manure with peat and topsoil. If soil is heavily clayey, you can add builders' sharp sand to help open it up and provide improved drainage.

Next, place this improved soil mixture in the hole and position your tree or shrub. Details about actual planting are included in a later chapter. If you wish to renovate and improve soil for a bed of bulbs, flower garden, or vegetable- or fruit-growing area, you can double-dig or rototill deeply. Spread manure, peat, compost, and old mulch materials on the surface. As you dig with a spade, pile the first spadefuls in a line. Then dig a second level deeper and turn that over. Continue digging and mixing soil to achieve a deeper growing area that will provide an improved root zone for plant growth.

Rototillers are amazing and versatile tools. From simple and effective Toro Tillers to powerful Troy Bilt ones that dig and pulverize soil deeply, you can save time and labor with these power tools. Resist the urge to till or dig when soil is wet. You may damage the structure more than help it. Also resist the urge to thoroughly pulverize the soil. The best soil structure is a crumbly, fluffy, but not dusty condition. Tillers can be rented, too, and save both your back and hours of digging effort.

Plan to add mulch each year around shrubs and trees and on all garden areas as you have material available. Humus that you make in your own compost pile is an excellent mulch and soil additive along garden rows and around plants. Apply mulch 2 to 4 inches deep. Spread deeper layers of the lighter materials such as grass clippings and straw. They'll eventually settle down.

Feeding plants is easier than ever nowadays. Balanced garden fertilizers are available at supermarkets, garden centers, and nurseries nationwide. Bags list the nutrients included: nitrogen for vegetative growth of leaves and stems; phosphorus and potash for growth of roots, fruits, and flowers. Tree spikes and simple hose-end attachments let you apply nutrients beneath the soil surface to roots of trees and shrubs. The directions on the packages provide the details on how to feed your plantscape plants well and how often, too.

Remember several points. If you eat too much, you don't feel right. The same is true with plants. Overfeeding can encourage excessive growth, which means more pruning work for you. You also may encourage softer wood and stem development that is likely to suffer winterkill in harsh winters. Plants enjoy a balanced diet, so feed them only what they need, according to the label directions on the fertilizer you use.

You can improve garden areas bit by bit, year by year. It pays to improve the soil for the most permanent parts of your landscape, the trees and shrubs, first. That gives them the beneficial root zones they need to spread and grow well. Then, as you add other plants, from bulbs to perennials, and smaller ground covers to annual flower gardens, you can continue your soil-improvement practices. As you build better growing conditions in the good earth, your plants will take root more happily and reward you with a lovelier landscape as they thrive in the good earth.

Masses of tulips line a walk with color.

3.

Plan for Lovelier Living

The first step toward the lovelier landscape you want and deserve is easy. Begin with a pencil, graph paper, a ruler or T square, and the design symbols in this chapter. You'll find it lots easier to move the design on paper than to try transplanting a 15-foot tree that you planted in the wrong place on your home grounds. Landscape designing, like rearranging furniture, is much easier on your back when you use graph paper to map out the plans first.

The sketches in this chapter can be traced or copied. They represent the symbols used by landscape designers and horticulturists. Some are hedges, others shrubs, or deciduous or evergreen trees. You can, of course, make up your own. Your plan doesn't require fancy sketches or blueprints, either. However, by thinking ahead and putting ideas on paper, you'll be better able to visualize each step of your plantscape progress. Besides, a pencil and eraser are easier to use than a shovel and wheelbarrow.

There are five basic steps to successful landscaping. The first is to develop a list of existing and desired outdoor features. The second is to draw a base plan. Then you should outline major landscape features in general. After that, locate desired features in their proper landscape areas. Finally, plot your finished landscape plan so it can serve you well as a guide as you dig in to plant trees, shrubs, ground covers, beds, and borders that will give you that more attractive, happier outdoor environment you seek.

The outdoor features depend on your family needs and desires. This may include a patio for entertaining, a children's play area, or a sport and game living room outdoors.

If you like indoor bouquets, plan for a cutting garden of flowers. If you want to lower your food budget, plot in a vegetable garden area. List tool sheds, storage, and fruit plantings if you wish to enjoy tastier, sweeter living. Add other features, from backyard pool to greenhouse area. Then rearrange the list in order of priorities, starting with the things you want first. Since trees and shrubs can be growing while you accomplish other jobs, it's best to put them first on your priority activity list.

From your list, consider these basic principles for home landscaping: Drives and walks should be straight, unless you have good reason for curving them. If possible, put driveway and walk together to avoid breaking up other lawn and garden areas, especially your front lawn. A sweep of lawn and plants is more appealing than a concrete path from street to front door that detracts from the natural-living look.

Study homes that you admire. Notice that the most attractively landscaped homes use trees to frame the house and provide background for it, too. Don't block views with trees if possible.

Locate play areas, and utility areas especially, where they won't detract from the beauty of your home. Adults and children can grow together, but excess activity on lawns and into gardens can detract from your desired landscape look.

Avoid overplanting. Consult local nurseries, read mail-order nursery catalogs. Learn about the size, shape, and growth habits of trees and shrubs. Some may look just right now, but can overgrow your house or overshadow it. In general, tall houses need taller trees. Ranch-style and low, split-level modern homes look better with smaller or medium-size trees.

Grow most plants in beds and borders. You can achieve glorious displays of massed colors and contrasts, too, in beds and borders. The uninterrupted lawn sweeping to shrubs and trees around your home yields a look of spaciousness. It is also easier to mow and tend.

Balanced landscapes are usually better. Try to avoid one heavily planted area while another is sparsely planted. Another key point is blending. Not everything should have equal interest. You can create a center of interest with specimen plants if you wish. However, too many striking trees or plants will look more like a botanical collection, rather than a blend of loveliness that complements your home.

Add a variety of textures with different types of plants. Some plants have dense foliage or are dark and bushy. Others are light and airy. Consider foliage and bloom as well as size, shape, color, and texture. Then aim to blend these different natural tones and textures into the most pleasing picture possible. Coarse textures and plants with dense foliage will be dominant and should be used sparingly.

Borders are important, too. You can define property lines and assure yourself of greater privacy with fences, screens, or hedges. Fruitful hedges add up to tastier living.

Look at barren walls, stark views, unsightly areas. Think how to screen them from view with hedges, taller shrubs, low-growing evergreen trees, or other more decorative shrubs.

Walk around your property at all times of the day. Observe where the sun shines best and where it hardly ever reaches. You must plan for those plants that will thrive in the conditions that you have. You can change soil conditions, but the house is going to stay where it is.

Shrubs and small trees can be effective to break long lines and provide more graceful flow to your total design. Use only small shrubs near the door, and larger ones in corners or the ends of the house to soften harsh angles and corners. Consider where downspouts may create soggy ground. Then remind yourself to change that water flow or the type of plant to be grown there.

Berries on bushes and shrubs add color to the late-summer and fall landscape. Birds enjoy this thoughtfulness, too.

Some plants are brightly colored in their blooming time or with fall foliage. Too much color isn't good. You lose the striking effect of several bright plants that would be standouts if they had quieter backgrounds to enhance their own display.

Remember that you live in four seasons that vary, depending on the area of the country. Consider how your plants will appear in spring, summer, fall, and winter. You may wish to emphasize evergreens to give life to bleaker winter scenes. You may find the lists in this book even more helpful to guide you in planting for flowering displays from spring until fall frost. Proper choice of flowers, trees, and shrubs will allow you to enjoy everything that nature has to offer, any way you desire to apply it.

Once you have walked your land enough, and have compiled the elements you wish to add or change, it's graph, pencil, and ruler time.

You may wish to make the plan to scale right at the start, but it isn't really necessary. Draw a base plan as shown in the sketches in this chapter. It should include your property line, house location, and outbuildings, from garage or barn to sheds or storage areas. Be sure to mark utilities, both above and below ground. There's nothing worse than locating a new tree where it may look fine, but when you dig, you hit a power, water, or sewer line. Include all existing plant materials, trees, shrubs, and gardens. Add walks and drives, and such key graphic features as rocks, streams, wet areas, and other characteristics of the grounds.

Try to follow realistic proportions. Indicate dimensions right on the plan. This then becomes your base for future drawings, which you should do on tracing paper over the basic plan.

Measure property lines and boundaries. This avoids planting valuable trees or plants on a neighbor's land. Add your house and all buildings and structures.

For the next step, get some tracing paper that you can see through—it's available at stationery stores. Place this over your base plan. Sketch in the approximate location of major landscape areas. You may wish a living area where you plan to build a patio. Rough out in general contours the other major areas.

The public area is the way your home looks to friends, neighbors, guests, and passersby. It should be relatively simple and should combine with the rest of the neighborhood.

The service area is simple to plan. It should be out of sight, with provisions for screening it from view. It might include a place for garbage cans, tool or storage shed, cold frames, and compost piles. Plan how to screen them with hedges, shrubs, or perhaps fences.

Your private living area is your outdoor living room. This is the most important area and deserves careful attention. You may wish a patio or pool someday. Plan for it now. Perhaps you like to barbecue and eat outdoors. A screen house to avoid insects may be in order. If you enjoy glorious flowers, plot in where perennials will give you your fill of blooming beauty every year. Add a cutting garden or fruitful plants to let you reach out and savor the tasty rewards of a multipurpose landscape.

Next step: place a second tracing paper over your base plan. Add more details. Revise locations of play areas, flower beds, specimen trees, shrub borders. Erase what you don't like and try again. Or start with a totally different approach and vary your landscape plan. Then compare notes with your family and friends. It's much easier to change plans this way than dig out a planted mistake later.

You may find you want too many features, which will create a cluttered, crowded landscape. Go back to your priority list and decide which ones must go. You may realize, as you look at this stage of your plan, that budget limitations won't permit you to have all you want. Change priorities if necessary. Put emphasis on the permanent parts—trees and shrubs that will be growing taller and more beautiful as you fill in other details of your plan year by year.

This step of revision may take time. It does let you explore ways you can utilize your home grounds to best advantage. You may discard the idea of a storage shed and opt for a potting shed and greenhouse that are more versatile. You may realize that a windbreak is more important in this energy-conscious era to reduce cold winds that suck heat from your home. Make your changes on paper as many times as you wish. Eventually, you'll get a feel of what is most important to you and where you want to position your key elements for more enjoyable outdoor living.

The next step is the more detailed final plan. Use graph paper. Carefully sketch in the present permanent structures and existing features you wish to maintain. Then sketch in the areas and features you wish to add or alter: gardens, pool, patio, play area, miniorchard, vegetable-growing area. This provides you with an estimate of space available in relation to other items in your plan. With the graph paper divided into squares, you can now see clearly how much space each area will take. Allow a foot per square to get a more detailed view of your final landscape look.

Now you are coming to the finish line, the final, detailed, right-to-scale landscape plan. You can trace or copy the designs in this book to make a professional-looking plan if you wish.

Do the public area first. It will set your house off as one that welcomes friends and guests and says, "People that love plants live here."

Landscaping should blend your home into the surrounding area so it looks natural and comfortable. To accomplish this, soften strong vertical lines of the house with trees and shrubs. Trees will frame a house. They can add depth to it. Low homes look best with small- to medium-size trees that won't outgrow and dwarf the house. Bedded shrubs and border plantings create a transition from open lawn areas to the house itself. Your doorway where friends enter is the focal point for your public-area planting.

The types of plants you choose and use should lead a visitor's eye to the entrance. You can accomplish this by positioning larger plants at the corners of the house, graduating to smaller plants toward the door. Taller trees can be used to break the roof line, or if in the private backyard area, provide a natural, softer backdrop to your house when viewed from the street.

Additional details and samples of actual plans for various types of homes are included in this book. They are designed as guides to help you evaluate types of home styles and plantings that create exceptionally lovely landscape designs. You can, of course, vary any plan to suit your own needs and tastes. The plans that have been included for ranch, split-level, colonial, and other types of houses will help you visualize how you too can design attractive plantscapes of your own.

There is little that can be done with service areas, except to screen unsightly views. Consider fencing, hedges, and combinations that will be pleasing. Remem-

Hanging plants can provide a blooming welcome to your home.

ber to look beyond your own property. You may be tidy and your service areas well tended, but your neighbors may not have the same high standards as you do. Consider, as you plan, what views of their land you don't want to see. Then add screening features, from tall stockade fences on which you can grow roses or espalier shrubs from your side, to permanent plantings of fast-growing evergreens. As you plan, keep in mind that plants have more benefits than good looks. They screen out views, noise, soot, and dirt. They can reduce the wind-chill factor as well as provide shade for a sitting area. Trees are versatile, so think about their many functions.

As you plan a patio, watch the sun move through the sky. You can plant a tree where it will provide shade during the time of day you will normally use the patio. If you wish to sunbathe regularly, the reverse is true; avoid planting tall shade trees where they deprive you of your daily tanning time.

There is no real need to name specific plant materials as you make your plan. You can indicate simply coniferous or deciduous trees or use the stylized diagrams in this book.

Mark simply fruit trees or berry patches for ease, then decide later which type of fruit you wish to grow. Note the ground cover on the plan where you want it, then decide from catalogs or discussions with your local nurseryman or garden center which ones suit your desires best.

Put all features on paper to scale. You can look up in special books the mature size of trees not listed in this book. On your plan, draw in the mature size so you realize what your total scene will be when your plants and trees grow up, as they will do.

Once you have completed your landscape plan, make a copy on a copy machine. That's insurance that the dog won't eat the one and only copy, or a child tear it, or you spill coffee all over it and wash away the lines. Since you will be working with it regularly as you dig in and plant, either seal the master plan in plastic or encase it in a plastic envelope. That way, you can use grease pencil to indicate your progress.

As you develop your plan and plant accordingly, you can periodically use colored pencils to color in the completed features. Show fall foliage in appropriate colors and evergreens in their shades of green. Eventually, you will have an attractive color drawing for framing in the den, as well as a guide for future use.

DECIDUOUS TREES
AND SHRUBS

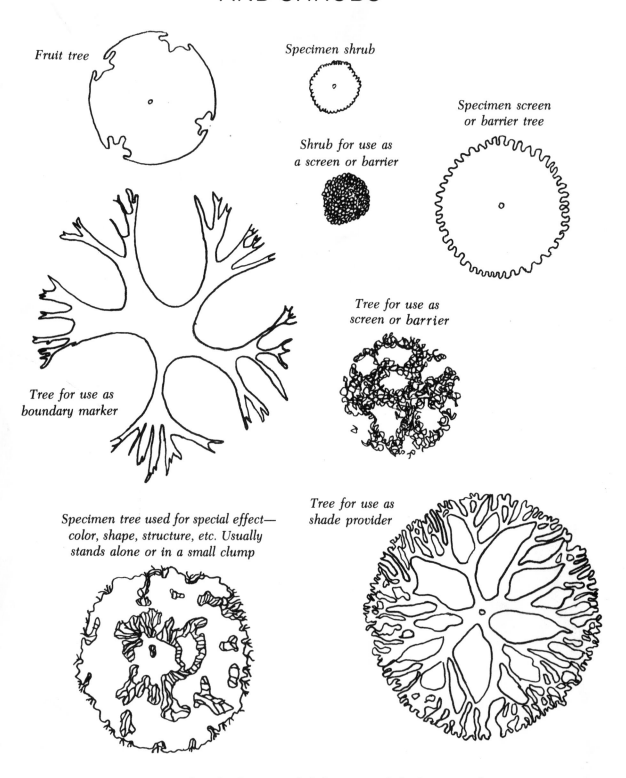

Fruit tree

Specimen shrub

Specimen screen or barrier tree

Shrub for use as a screen or barrier

Tree for use as screen or barrier

Tree for use as boundary marker

Tree for use as shade provider

Specimen tree used for special effect— color, shape, structure, etc. Usually stands alone or in a small clump

You can use these landscape symbols for trees and shrubs as you plan your own lovelier landscape. They are typical symbols used as indicated, but you can make up your own simpler designs as you wish.

EVERGREEN TREES
AND SHRUBS

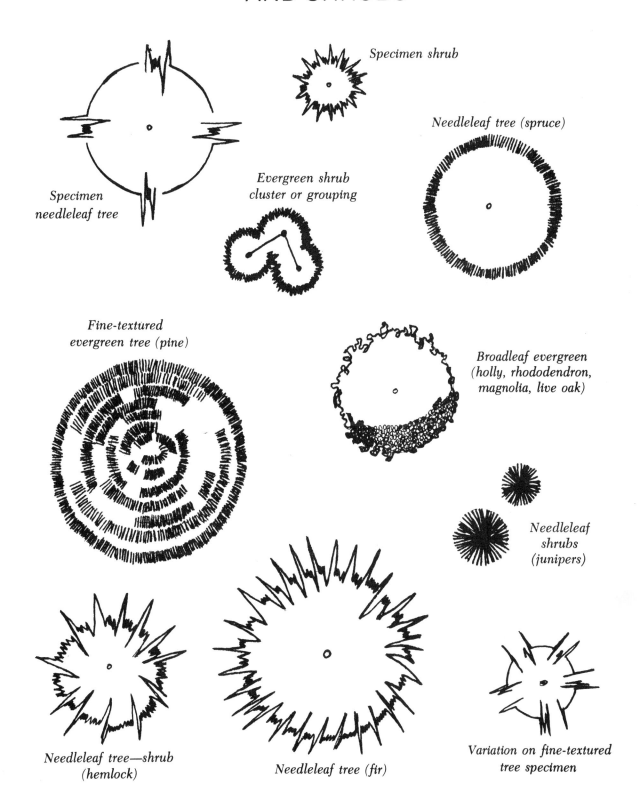

Specimen shrub

Evergreen shrub
cluster or grouping

Needleleaf tree (spruce)

Specimen
needleleaf tree

Fine-textured
evergreen tree (pine)

Broadleaf evergreen
(holly, rhododendron,
magnolia, live oak)

Needleleaf
shrubs
(junipers)

Needleleaf tree—shrub
(hemlock)

Needleleaf tree (fir)

Variation on fine-textured
tree specimen

Your front door should be plantscaped to welcome friends and guests to your home. In this design, a medium-sized tree flanks one side of the door while lower growing shrubs set off the entranceway. Yews and glossy leaf privet, holly and azalea, low growing cotoneaster provide a pleasing combination of evergreen and deciduous shrubs. You can combine others to achieve the same effect; a flow of harmonious shrub shapes, leaf size and textures that says welcome to your home.

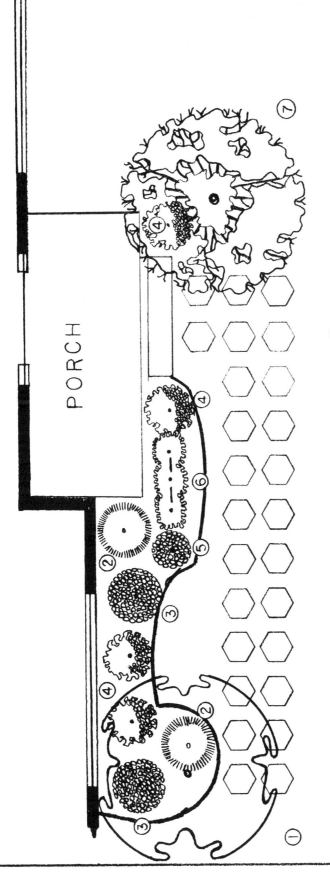

PORCH

FLAGSTONE
WALK

SCALE:

1" = 5'0"

Plant List

	Botanical Name	Common Name
1.	Crataegus coccinioides	Scarlet hawthorn
2.	Taxus media	English yew
3.	Ligustrum lucidum	Glossy-leaf privet
4.	Ilex crenata	Helleri holly
5.	Rhododendron indicum	Indica azalea
6.	Cotoneaster horizontalis	Rock cotoneaster
7.	Betula populifolia	Gray birch

A cluster of white birch trees are the focal point for this nicely private backyard garden setting. Pachysandra serves as a ground cover in the shady area beneath trees while perennials border the lawn. Azaleas, which prefer some shade, add splashes of color, are readily viewed from inside the home. Tulips and other spring flower bulbs can be utilized for early spring color, along with daffodils in a natural setting beneath the trees. You can vary this plantscape however you wish, keeping in mind the sun and shade requirements for the plants you select. Shady lawn seed mixtures often are necessary beneath large trees to provide the sweep of attractive, lush lawn grass which ties the whole landscape together.

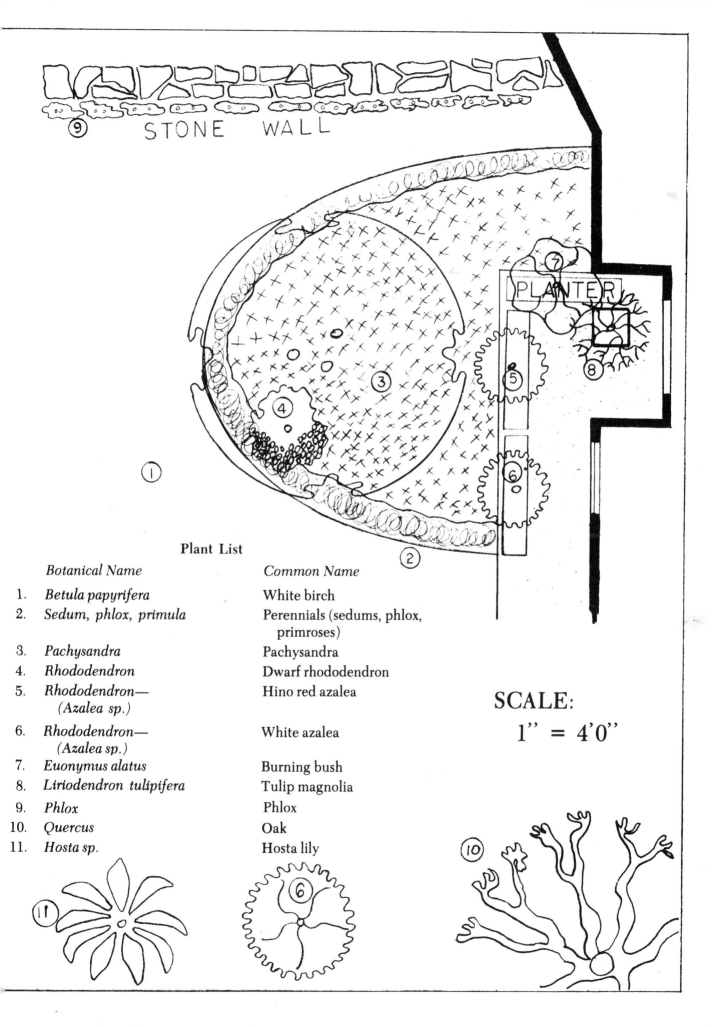

STONE WALL

Plant List

	Botanical Name	Common Name
1.	*Betula papyrifera*	White birch
2.	*Sedum, phlox, primula*	Perennials (sedums, phlox, primroses)
3.	*Pachysandra*	Pachysandra
4.	*Rhododendron*	Dwarf rhododendron
5.	*Rhododendron—* (*Azalea sp.*)	Hino red azalea
6.	*Rhododendron—* (*Azalea sp.*)	White azalea
7.	*Euonymus alatus*	Burning bush
8.	*Liriodendron tulipifera*	Tulip magnolia
9.	*Phlox*	Phlox
10.	*Quercus*	Oak
11.	*Hosta sp.*	Hosta lily

PLANTER

SCALE:
1" = 4'0"

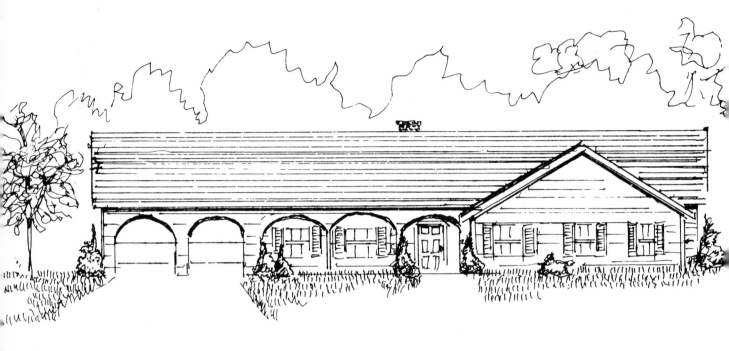

A long, low house calls for careful long-range planning. In this contemporary home, taller trees in the backyard and rear of the property provide a natural display of foliage to break up the roof line. Hemlocks which grow tall and somewhat pyramidal, can be planted to break up corner lines. They can be pruned periodically to retain a smaller size. Junipers, or arborvitae can be used as part of the front shrub plantings. You might also choose alternates such as yews, spreading or upright for the front plantings. Eventually, a flowering tree or two on the lawn can enhance the total living landscape picture with blooming beauty.

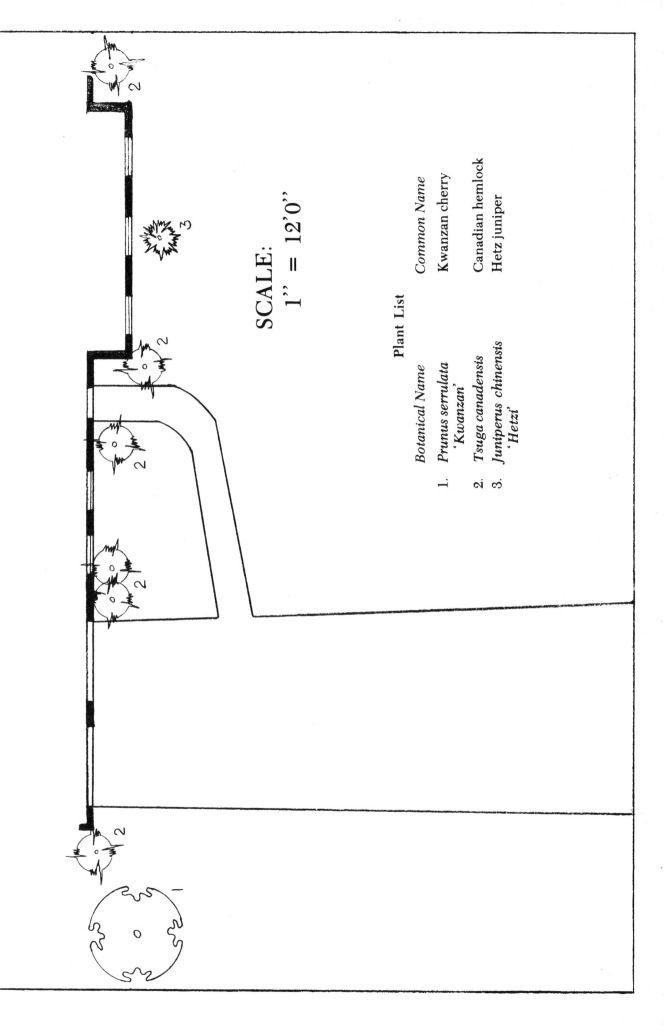

SCALE:
1" = 12'0"

Plant List

Botanical Name	Common Name
1. *Prunus serrulata* 'Kwanzan'	Kwanzan cherry
2. *Tsuga canadensis*	Canadian hemlock
3. *Juniperus chinensis* 'Hetzi'	Hetz juniper

Fallon 77

Landscaping a sloping entrance area should be no problem. A fire-thorn will thrive at the side of the drive. It can be trained to reach across over the garage door. Holly, yew or dwarf mugho pine can be used at the doorway with a grouping of shrubs including hemlock or several pyra-midal yews at the corner of the home. Taller evergreens from upright ar-borvitae to hemlocks might be your choice on the lower driveway level. You could elect to plant medium-size deciduous trees instead. If the slope is steep from door to drive, consider a rock garden or several terrac-ed levels. As an alternate, ground covers that hold soil, and reduce mow-ing chores are effective.

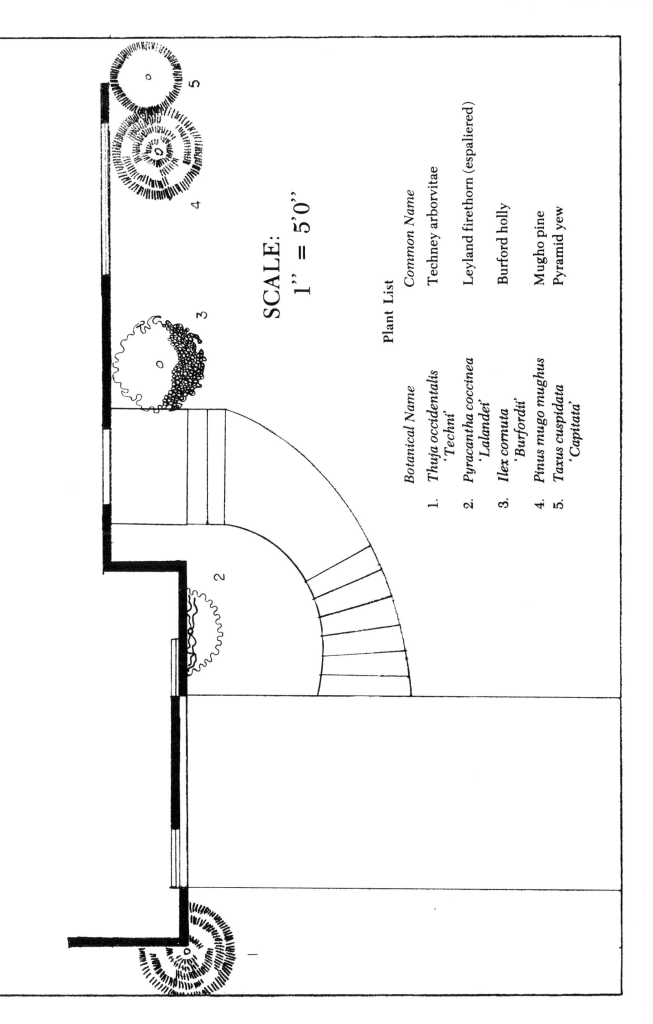

SCALE:
1" = 5'0"

Plant List

	Botanical Name	Common Name
1.	*Thuja occidentalis* 'Techni'	Techney arborvitae
2.	*Pyracantha coccinea* 'Lalandei'	Leyland firethorn (espaliered)
3.	*Ilex cornuta* 'Burfordii'	Burford holly
4.	*Pinus mugo mughus*	Mugho pine
5.	*Taxus cuspidata* 'Capitata'	Pyramid yew

Small homes can look mighty small and barren without landscaping. From this stark look of a newly-built home, you can create a lived-in and well-loved home look with this simple, basic landscape planting. Just a few trees and shrubs make all the difference and won't strain your budget.

Plant List

	Botanical Name	Common Name
1.	*Populus nigra* 'Italica'	Lombardy poplar
2.	*Malus floribunda*	Japanese flowering crab apple
3.	*Viburnum rhytidophyllum*	Leatherleaf viburnum
4.	*Juniperus chinensis* 'Pfitzeriana'	Pfitzer's juniper
5.	*Rhododendron* 'P.J.M. Hybrids'	PJM rhododendron
6.	*Thuja occidentalis*	Dark American arborvitae

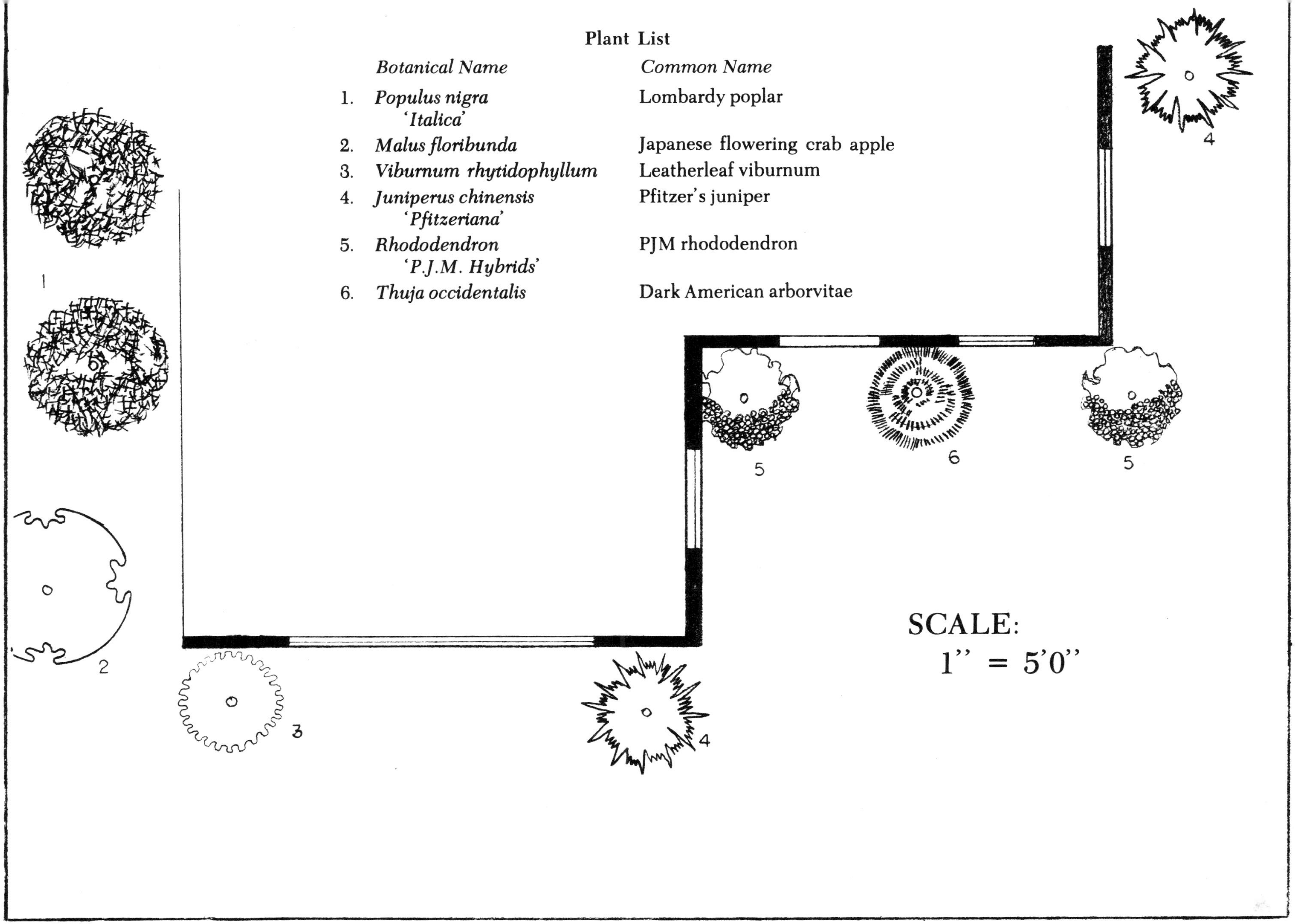

SCALE:
1" = 5'0"

Fellon 77

Trees at the corner of a home extend the size of a small house while giving it a neatly landscaped look. Lower shrubs beneath windows draw the eye to the entrance. Beware of buying tall growing shrubs that will eventually, and often quickly, grow up to hide your home. In all landscaping plans, remember that some shrubs require regular pruning. Others are naturally dwarf and save you time and work. Your local nursery can provide valuable advice on those that are most carefree.

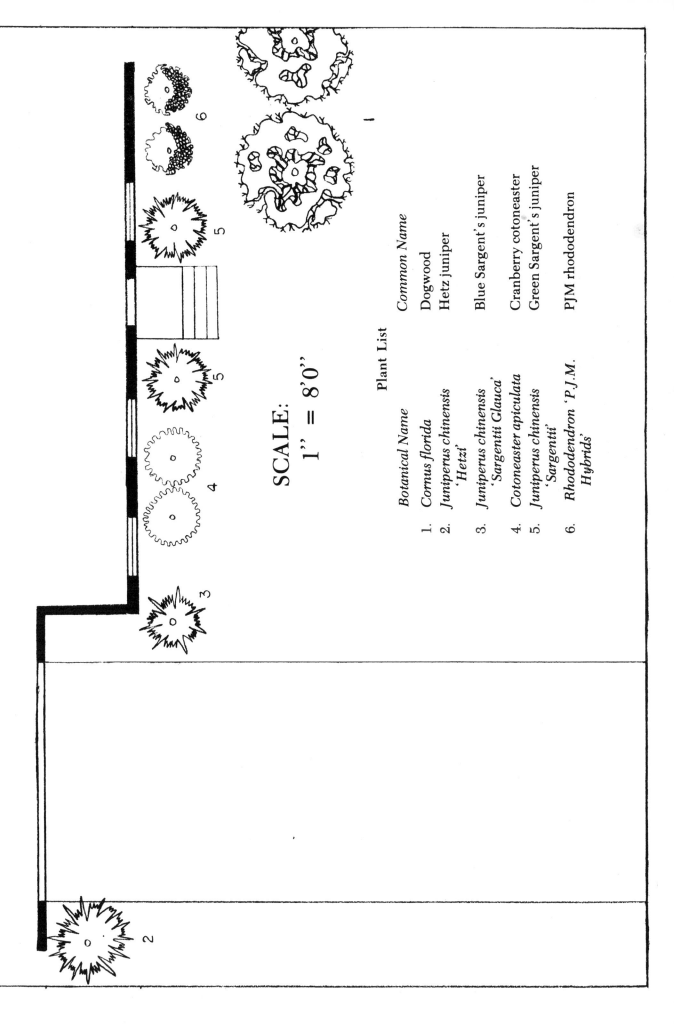

SCALE:
1" = 8'0"

Plant List

	Botanical Name	Common Name
1.	Cornus florida	Dogwood
2.	Juniperus chinensis 'Hetzi'	Hetz juniper
3.	Juniperus chinensis 'Sargentii Glauca'	Blue Sargent's juniper
4.	Cotoneaster apiculata	Cranberry cotoneaster
5.	Juniperus chinensis 'Sargentii'	Green Sargent's juniper
6.	Rhododendron 'P.J.M. Hybrids'	PJM rhododendron

Fallon 77

Don't overcrowd a landscape plan. Just a few well chosen trees and shrubs will greatly improve your home's appearance. Those included in this plan can be varied as your taste and locale dictate. It is far better to underplant than create an overgrown jungle that hides the beauty of your home itself. Remember too, that trees and shrubs grow all around, not just upward. Plant them far enough from your foundation so painting and building maintenance can be accomplished properly.

Plant List

	Botanical Name	Common Name
1.	*Aesculus octandra*	Buckeye
2.	*Aesculus hippocastanum carnea*	Red horse chestnut
3.	*Thuja occidentalis nigra*	Dark American arborvitae
4.	*Thuja occidentalis 'Woodwardi'*	Globe arborvitae
5.	*Rhododendron 'Nova Zemble'*	Nova zembla rhododendron
6.	*Taxus cuspidata densiforma*	Densiforma yew
7.	*Chamaecyparis obtusa*	Hinoka cypress
8.	*Juniperus chinensis 'Hetzi'*	Hetz juniper
9.	*Wisteria sinensis*	Chinese wisteria

SCALE:
1" = 6'0"

Landscaping a Small Property

If you have a small, regularly sized lot, you should aim your landscape plans to do two things: first, to provide an attractive and natural setting for the house; and second, to provide an attractive, private outdoor living room for your family fun.

Follow the step-by-step procedures already explained in this chapter by laying out the initial paper plan and adding the initial structures. Then combine the best of trees, shrubs, flowers, and vegetables to provide yourself with the most attractive outdoor environment. The first rule is to keep things simple. Landscaping doesn't mean building a plant collection. That's the job of an arboretum. The second key point: plan wisely, with your list of priorities and wants firmly in mind. Third, put your plan on paper, vary it, and finally decide what you wish to achieve as the total look of your homestead.

Since trees provide shade and beauty, bloom and fall foliage, and design features to serve as accents or complements for your home, position them where they will look best to you. Many books have been written about the value of lawns, how to start, renovate, feed, weed, and care for them. Lawn building is not a purpose of this book. Scotts, the lawn people, have many more tips and ideas than we could possibly put into this book. They also have the reliable seed and products to assure you a luxurious, weed-free lawn.

The lawn is, of course, the foundation or carpet on which you build your living landscape. To maintain a healthy, green, weed-free lawn requires regular fertilization and weed control. You must provide adequate water and mow properly and often. The sweep of a lush green lawn to and around your home and grounds is a vital part of sensible, attractive landscaping.

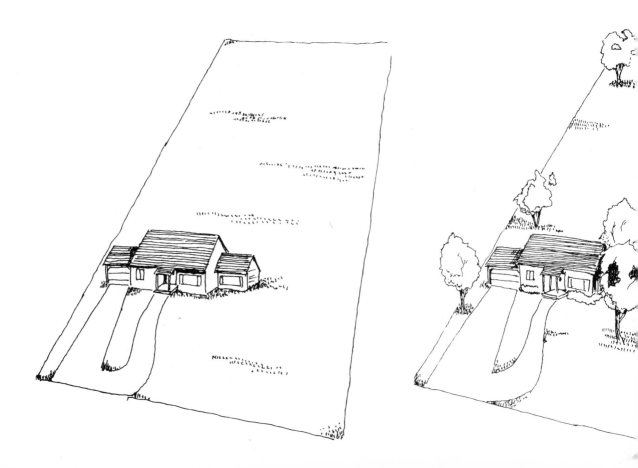

Your local garden center can guide you in the right, greener-growing directions. From the viewpoint of landscaping, lawns should be as open and uncluttered as possible. Avoid plantings within lawns that detract from the landscaping of your home. Also, avoid trees in lawns which will require more careful mowing and work. A small shade tree or colorful specimen may be appropriate, however, especially if it provides a pleasant sight through a picture window and helps block off street scenes. In general, shrub plantings look best along sides and borders of lawns and are easier to tend there as well.

Shade trees are best used to frame the house. They are nature's air conditioners, not only shading your home from the hot sun, but giving off ample moisture in their natural transpiration process. A large tree may release many gallons of moisture daily, which has a cooling effect on your environment.

How many and which trees you plant depends on the space you have and your own landscape judgment. You may plant medium trees within 20 to 25 feet of the house, but a good rule is only one or two, so they don't detract from your overall total landscape look.

If you have a long narrow lot, you can select smaller trees like dogwood, hawthorn, or birch. Space them irregularly to produce a more natural, rather than starkly formal look.

If you desire more shade, consider where the trees should be to cast their cooling shadows on your home. In this design, we began with the house and lot. The first step was trees for shade and to be the frame for the home. This house faces north. Trees used for shade are at the back, so they provide desired shade and privacy. You'll notice that these backyard trees also function effectively to break up the house's long roof line.

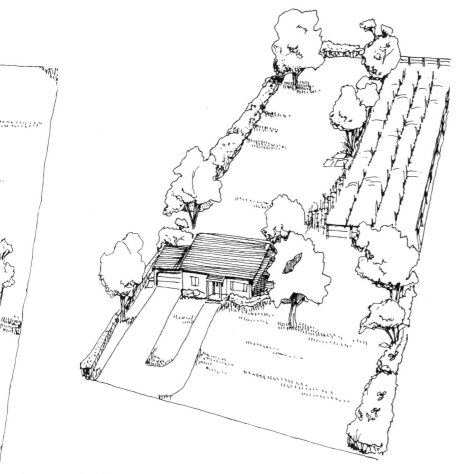

These sketches show the step-by-step development of a complete, well-planned landscape. Detailed plans start on the next page.

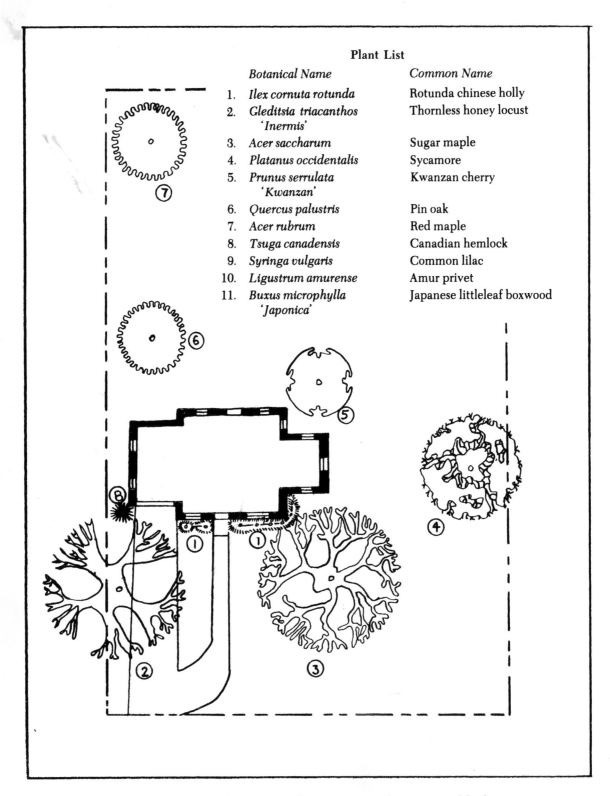

Plant List

	Botanical Name	Common Name
1.	*Ilex cornuta rotunda*	Rotunda chinese holly
2.	*Gleditsia triacanthos* 'Inermis'	Thornless honey locust
3.	*Acer saccharum*	Sugar maple
4.	*Platanus occidentalis*	Sycamore
5.	*Prunus serrulata* 'Kwanzan'	Kwanzan cherry
6.	*Quercus palustris*	Pin oak
7.	*Acer rubrum*	Red maple
8.	*Tsuga canadensis*	Canadian hemlock
9.	*Syringa vulgaris*	Common lilac
10.	*Ligustrum amurense*	Amur privet
11.	*Buxus microphylla* 'Japonica'	Japanese littleleaf boxwood

On a small suburban or city lot, you can achieve a world of privacy, greenery and good growing fun. This plan is scaled 1 inch to 20 feet. Initially shade and flowering trees were planted so they could be growing larger as the rest of the landscape design was planted into its planned place. A sugar maple adds its graceful form as well as brilliant fall color. A sycamore, with its unique bark and welcome shade, helps screen the neighbor's house. A pin oak, and red maple also serve to vary form and style of trees in the landscape. Kwanzan cherry trees blaze with color

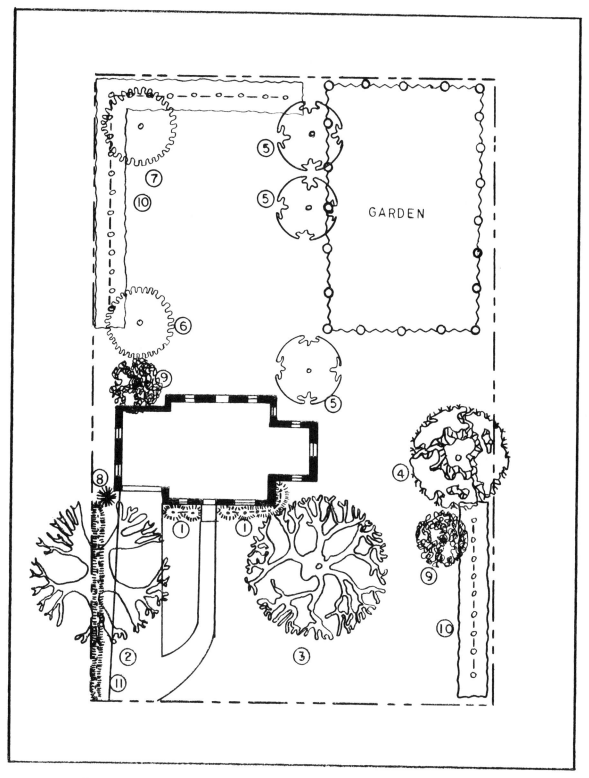

each spring as specimens near the future backyard garden area.

As the plan is planted, a hemlock helps to screen one side of the property, while lilacs are used to provide privacy on the other side of the lot. These also yield beautiful spring displays as they perfume the air. Additional privacy is insured with a privet hedge along the rear property line as it helps enclose your private outdoor living area. Eventually, a vegetable garden, complete with berry bushes can be completed in the opposite corner to produce tasty abundance in a small lot landscape plan.

As you consider the best and most striking or functional trees, look over the diagrams. There are three types of trees and shrubs. Deciduous ones shed their leaves in fall and grow new ones each spring. Conifers are evergreens such as pines, with their typical needles, or firs and spruces. Broadleaf evergreens are plants such as rhododendrons, whose leaves remain on the plant all year round.

Shape also has a bearing on your landscape design. Some trees are round, others oval, pyramidal, or weeping. The sketches here reveal how different shapes can alter the look of a landscape.

Once you have made your initial sketches over your base plan, add in the details. In this design, shade trees frame and set off the home. Property line hedges provide privacy, which can be important on smaller city and suburban lots.

The foundation planting in the front public area, and around any side or rear sitting areas, help "anchor" the house in a natural setting. These low-growing shrubs soften the architectural lines. They should be in proper proportion to the size of your home. You can select evergreens like junipers, yews, and rhododendrons, or blend them with deciduous shrubs or even fruitful ones like currants or blueberries.

Avoid a plant-collection look of all individual types. Rather, use a few of each to achieve pleasing balance, with variations in form, texture, shape, and growth habit.

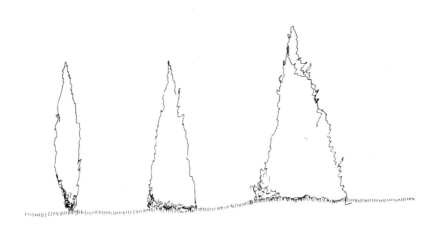

Trees and shrubs grow to their own special shape and forms. These silhouettes can help you as you design your landscape. Local nurserymen can match the specific tree variety to the shape and symmetry you want.

You may prefer highly stylized, constantly pruned specimens. If that's your desire, fine. In general, these overly formal plantings look too stark and stiff. They also require constant pruning care.

How you design your private backyard living room depends on your likes and activities. This design includes a play and family area just outside a family-room door. A patio is intended in the future and perhaps a pool. Flower beds border the vegetable garden, which provides, along with fruit trees, the tastier living that can reward you from even a small home landscape plan.

Revitalize an Old, Overgrown Home

Many people prefer the grace and charm of an older home. Fact is, older houses often are less expensive and provide more living space than new ones. If you are faced with a landscape that is elderly and overgrown, take heart. Renovation, pruning, removal, and replacement can revitalize that crowded landscape.

The first step begins on paper, plotting in all existing structures, driveway, walks, and other key features of the property as shown in Figure A. This home has unique plants to be preserved and restored to health. It also needs a plantscaping face-lift.

Before you put axe, saw, and pruning shears into action, complete your paper plan. Overgrown lilacs can be transplanted to yield new gardens full, if you don't get overanxious and axe them all away.

The second phase of the design is shown in Figure B. All existing trees and shrubs are placed as they appear on the land. When first planted they may have looked quite lovely. Volunteer maples eventually grew up through a privet hedge. Yews overgrew in all directions. Storms damaged weak-wooded trees. Privet, once around a formal sitting yard, became a 15-foot-tall jumble, hiding the arbor and crowding out roses climbing over graceful trellis arches.

The third phase of this revitalization landscape plan reveals on paper where additions were added. After pruning to bring yews, juniper, privet, and mugho pines back into attractive, lower-growing balance, tall "weed" trees were eliminated. Dead wood was removed from old and overgrown trees.

A rock garden was added on the rear driveway on a sloping area that was difficult to mow. Ground covers were utilized, well mulched as overspreading shrubs were pruned back to realistic, balanced size.

The land behind the old home slopes to the rear. A sitting area with repruned privet is screened effectively from roadside traffic noises. Around the hedges, perennial flower beds were added to provide color against the dark-green privet foliage. Fruit trees were positioned behind a woven colonial-style fence for a fruitful touch of tastier living.

Along the property border, daffodils, iris, day lilies, and other perennials against the privet hedge are colorful visual treats to be seen from dining room, den, and upstairs bedrooms. Behind the flagpole on the driveway lawns, peonies and annuals in an arch provide a decorative display as guests arrive.

Much must still be done to bring these gardens back to their fullest potential. But with a basic plan on paper and a reasonable annual budget, this home and others like it are being restored to the elegant displays of trees, shrubs, flowers and beautiful growing loveliness.

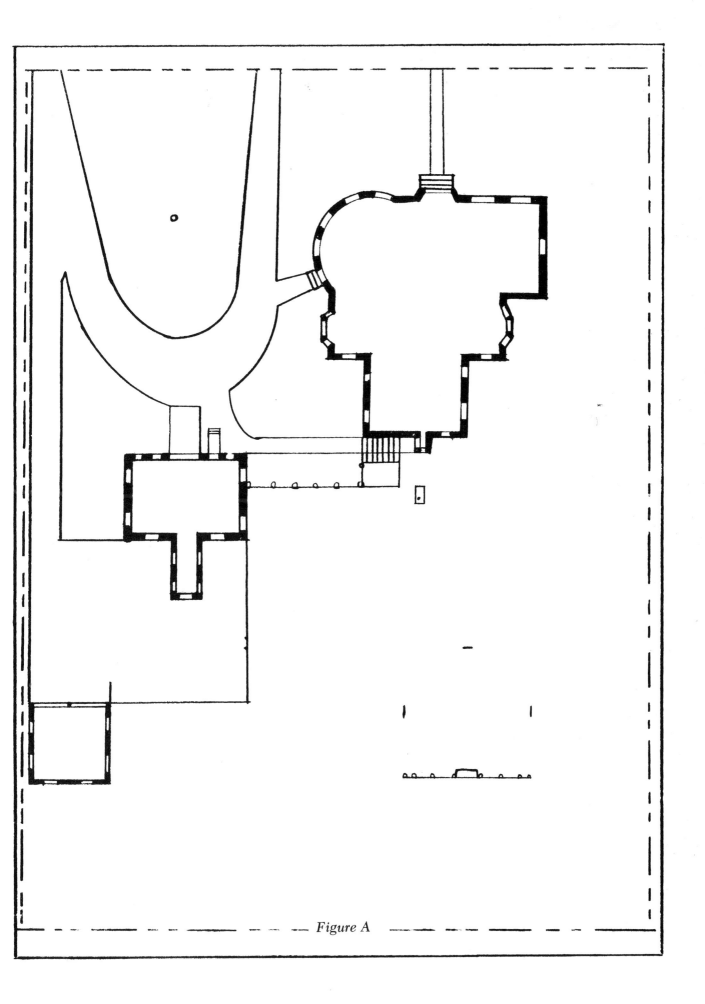

Figure A

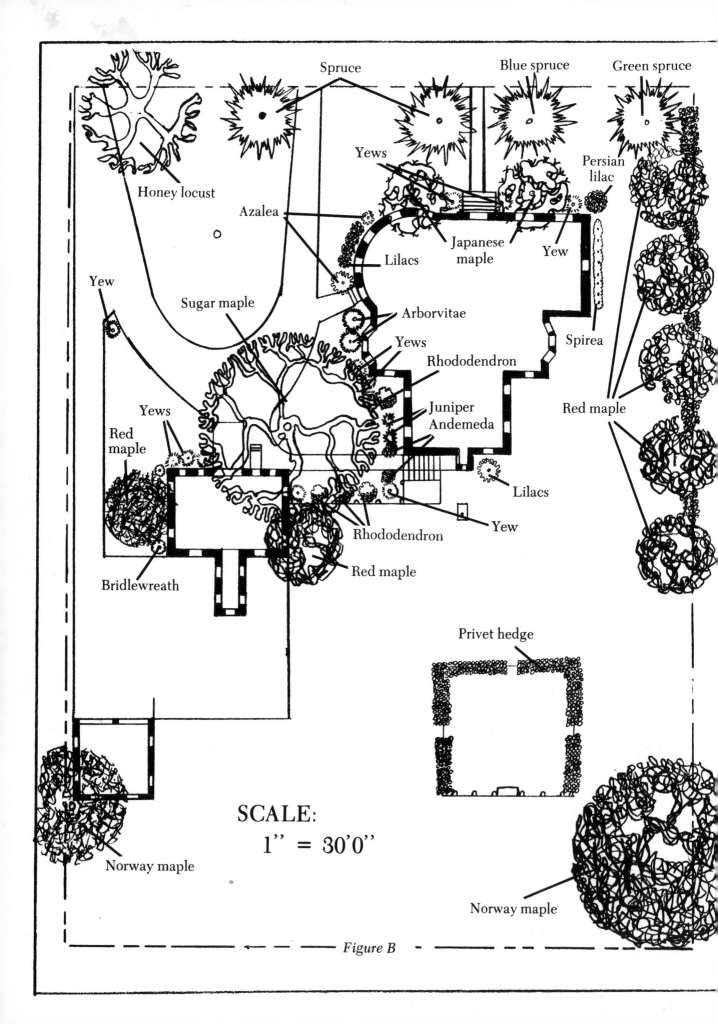

Honey locust

Spruce

Blue spruce

Green spruce

Yews

Azalea

Persian lilac

Japanese maple

Yew

Yew

Sugar maple

Lilacs

Arborvitae

Spirea

Yews

Rhododendron

Red maple

Juniper
Andemeda

Yews

Red
maple

Red maple

Lilacs

Rhododendron

Yew

Bridlewreath

Red maple

Privet hedge

Norway maple

SCALE:
1'' = 30'0''

Norway maple

Figure B

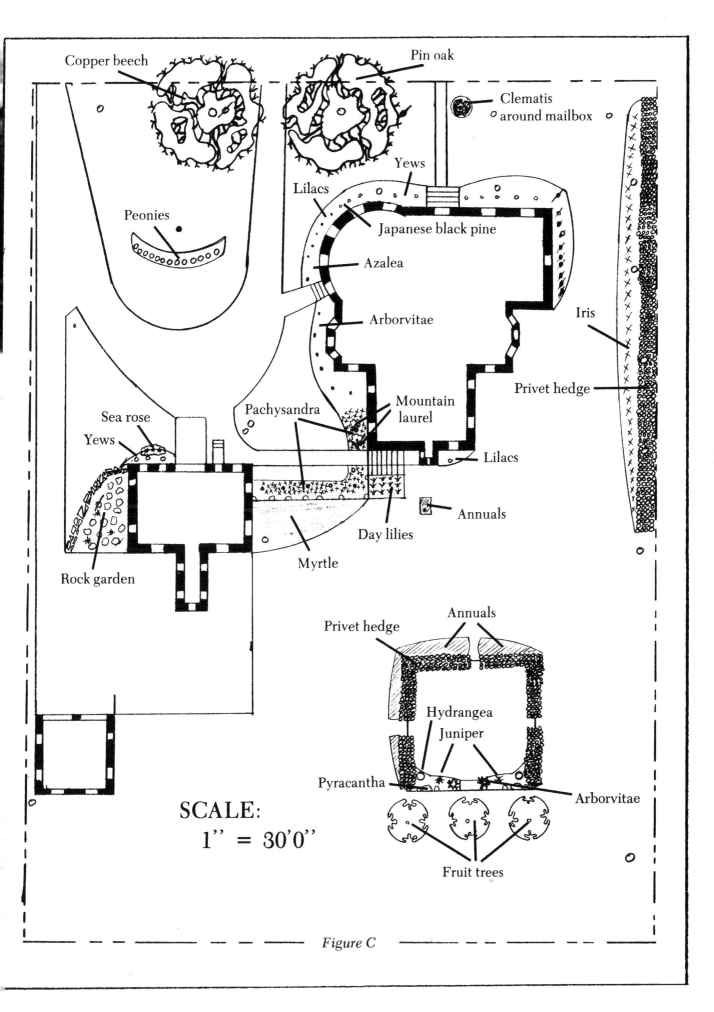

Copper beech

Pin oak

Clematis around mailbox

Peonies

Lilacs

Yews

Japanese black pine

Azalea

Arborvitae

Iris

Sea rose

Pachysandra

Mountain laurel

Privet hedge

Yews

Lilacs

Rock garden

Annuals

Myrtle

Day lilies

Privet hedge

Annuals

Hydrangea

Juniper

Pyracantha

Arborvitae

Fruit trees

SCALE:
1'' = 30'0''

Figure C

4.

How to Plant

Trees and shrubs are a permanent part of your home plantscape. It pays to plant them properly so they establish a strong, sturdy roothold. They'll reward you with lasting loveliness for many years.

Soil improvement is the first key step. Proper planting is the second key to more beautiful home grounds. Too often many people merely dig a hole. Then they wonder why their investment doesn't thrive. Considering that trees and shrubs will be in their new home ground for years to come, a little extra time spent in planting is well worth while.

You can buy landscaping plants from many sources: local nurseries, garden centers, or by mail from nurseries. At the end of this book you will find a list of reputable firms that have a wide range of beautiful specimens of all types available. You can transplant wild native trees, but that's risky. The secret is twofold: first, removing a sufficiently large root ball and soil; and second, matching the location and growing conditions to what the plant had and needed in its native habitat. Usually, nursery-grown, pruned, and healthy trees are a much wiser choice.

Landscape plants are offered bare root or B and B, which means balled and burlapped. Bare root should be planted in the dormant period, before leaves form in spring or after they have dropped in fall. Balled and burlapped plants are dug with a root intact in a ball of soil, wrapped in a square of burlap, and secured with twine or wire ties.

Nurseries and garden centers especially also sell plants in metal, fiber, or plastic containers. Container-grown and B-and-B plants are a better bet. They may cost slightly more, but they can be planted any time except during icy winters. They don't usually suffer from transplanting shock as bare-root trees may. They are, of course, slightly higher in price.

Spring and fall are the best planting times. Summer is usually too hot, which leads to excess moisture loss. Early spring, while plants are not actively growing, is the best season for planting or transplanting most evergreen and deciduous shrubs and trees. Bare-root plants, mainly available from mail-order firms, should be planted only in early spring or autumn while fully dormant.

Spring planting gives hard-to-start plants the longest possible growing season to establish roots in the new location. Azalea, beech, birch, most broadleaf evergreens, dogwood, hemlock, magnolia, and oaks are the most common trees that need time to set a firm roothold.

Fall planting time begins in September. Narrow-leaved evergreens may be transplanted then, when the summer's growth has matured. They should not be planted later, because the roots may not have sufficient time to establish themselves before the ground freezes.

Most hardy, nonevergreen plants can be set during fall after the leaves have dropped, right until frozen ground makes digging impractical.

Americans are accustomed to instant results—the "TV dinner" syndrome. In landscaping, the cost of full-size specimens is usually prohibitive. Large plants also are more difficult to establish. More important, however, smaller-sized trees have youthful vigor. They recover from transplanting more quickly and grow at a more rapid rate. A smaller tree often outgrows a larger one over a period of years.

Another fact of plant life to consider is adaptability of the type of tree or shrub to its new location. Most broadleaf evergreens and some deciduous plants suffer winter injury from full exposure to winter sun and sweeping winds. If possible, use them in protected or partially shaded northern and eastern sides of buildings. Anti-wilt sprays also are available to prevent needles from drying out the first critical year in their new location. These sprays coat needles with a protective covering. When spring growth begins, the coating falls off.

Roots are the foundation of your plants. Whether you choose bare root or B and B, keep the roots or root ball protected. Never allow roots to dry out, even for a short period. If plants arrive before you can plant them, dig a trench and place the roots in it, covered with soil. This "heeling in" procedure protects precious roots. Keep soil moist, of course.

When you are ready to plant, really dig in. Make the hole deep enough to set the plant at the same level at which it originally grew. Dig the hole wider than the root ball or container and large enough so bare-root plants roots can spread naturally, with a little room to spare.

As you dig the holes, place topsoil in one pile, subsoil in another. Laying plastic or canvas on the ground first makes cleanup easier. If subsoil is poor, replace it with a combination planting mixture of equal parts of topsoil, peat moss, and composted humus. Around new homes, foundation backfill may be rocky and filled with debris. If so, replace it to provide the best possible growing conditions for new plants.

Handle plants carefully. Don't drop root balls into holes, because you will damage roots and their fine root hairs. Leave the burlap in place after untying it. It will decay in the ground. Roots can grow through it anyway. If the root ball is firm and fibrous, you can remove the burlap for other uses. Cut sides of fiber containers or remove metal ones carefully. Gently place the root ball in the hole. If you don't have at least 6 inches around the root ball or bare roots, take the plant out and dig the hole larger.

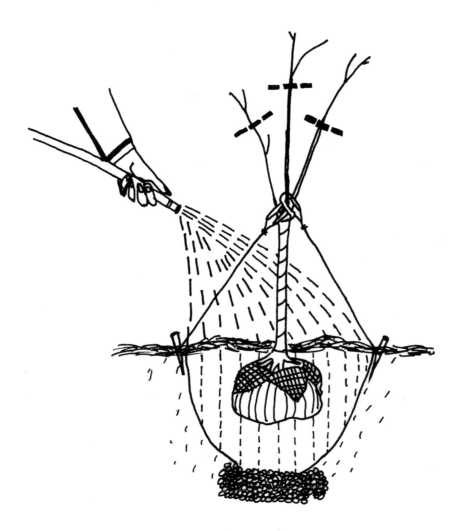

Many trees are available balled and burlapped. It pays to take the time to plant them well so they get a proper roothold for many years of healthy growth. Place the plant, root ball intact in the hole. Add soil around it to fill half the hole. Tamp down and water well. Add more soil to fill the hole, tamp it down and soak the soil. Remove any broken or damaged branches by cutting back to healthy wood. Mulching well will help retain soil moisture. Roots will grow through the burlap as it decomposes, but do open the top area if it is tightly around the trunk.

Next, work soil around the base of the ball firmly. Use a blunt stick or your fist. Plants should set securely in place. Then add more soil around the ball to fill the hole half full. Add water slowly to soak the soil. Let it settle well all around the roots. Then add the remaining soil and tamp firmly into place. Water well again.

Leave a saucer-shaped basin around your newly planted tree or shrub. This catches rain to direct moisture where newly started roots can find it. Level the area before winter so ice doesn't accumulate, if you live in northern areas.

Mulch next. Compost or wood chips, old leaves, or similar organic material can be used. This will help smother weeds, prevent soil moisture loss, and save work. Organic mulch also slowly decays to help improve soil condition.

Pruning is important, too. Despite careful handling, some branches may be broken. You also will disturb or damage some roots. Compensate for this by cutting back long branches, any damaged ones, and shaping the tree or bush to a desired shape.

If you plant acid-loving shrubs, especially rhododendrons and azaleas, it's better to mulch with pine bark, pine needles, or oak leaves. They increase soil acidity, which these plants crave.

For the first year, go easy on fertilizer. Organic matter such as well-rotted compost and leaf mold is sufficient to improve soil and provide small amounts of nutrients. It is best, in general, to hold off using fertilizer until the year after planting. That avoids the risk of root burning. After that, root feeding with tree-food spikes or spreading tree and shrub fertilizer on the surface and watering in will be satisfactory. Always follow label directions. Too much food for plants is worse than too little. Plants don't enjoy overeating any more than you do.

Young trees may need staking to prevent swaying or tipping in heavy winds, ice storms, or harsh weather. If they move much, roots can be harmed.

Support small trees with a single stake placed a few inches from the trunk. Fasten the sapling to it with wide cloth tape or wire rope encased in rubber hose to avoid bark injury.

Guy larger trees in a triangular pattern. Use three equally spaced wires running from just above the lower branches to stakes in the ground several feet out from the trunk. Also encase these wires around the tree in rubber or plastic hose, to avoid bark injury. For close-in, sturdier support, use two stakes instead of one, or the triangular bracing method.

This gate effect of older landscape plants at a doorway and the corners of a home may have appeal to some, but as plants overgrow, they tend to accentuate sharp house lines rather than soften them.

This "V" effect shows how taller shrubs or small trees at the corner with lower growing ones near the door focus eye attention to the entranceway.

In general, you should select plants for the entrance area that do not grow too large. A tall house, however, may require somewhat larger shrubs to provide a proper balance of the structure and plants.

5.

Basic Landscape Think Points

Picking just the right tree for the right spot sounds easy, but deserves careful attention. Take time to look around you. Trees offer a wide variety of sizes, shapes, colors, textures, and features, including flowers and fruits. Some grow tall and narrow; others spread out. Some are short and hug the ground; others almost cascade. The size and shape you need depends on where you want the tree and what effect you wish to create. The illustrations show some of the shapely effects trees can provide.

Along streets, you would usually want a tree with a high crown that won't obstruct the vision of people driving down the street. Any tree for your lawn should have branches high enough to walk under and mow under without stooping.

If you prefer flowering and fruiting trees, think about any extra cleanup chores. Apples, pears, and peaches taste good, but they require work with sprays to control insects and disease.

Ask your local nursery about mature size and growth habit. Will the tree you like contribute to a predominantly horizontal or a vertical effect? Will it complement or contrast with existing plantings in shape or color? Perhaps it will form a conversational group with another plant, or serve as background for flowers and colorful ornamental plantings. You may want a striking specimen, such as a weeping cherry or mountain ash.

Many people prefer color in their landscape, a sparkle of sunlight from brilliant blooms in spring and bright foliage in the fall. Look over color catalogs from mail-order nurseries. They provide excellent reference material so you can visualize how trees and shrubs will look in your home grounds.

Spring color is the easiest to achieve. There are many more spring flowering plants available. Spring is, of course, nature's flowering time.

Although most trees and shrubs, as well as flowers, bloom in spring, you can arrange multiseason, long-blooming displays. The key to this is the choice of plants

Combining tall, medium and low plants creates an attractive corner planting that breaks the stark lines of the building.

A tall home needs a more massive corner planting and perhaps a large framing tree to set the home off well.

This planting is especially suitable for a corner window with ground covers that blend the planting together.

that bear their blossoms over extended periods, or choosing varieties that are showy in spring and summer into fall. A list in a later chapter will guide you in the selection of plants and the times they normally bloom. Careful selection from this list will let you enjoy more color every season of the year.

When you select plants, including trees, consider their effects in the fall as well as spring and summer; the effect of leaf form and texture, size, and shape as well as the growing pattern of the plant. For example, visualize how the red-leaved Japanese maple will appear, silhouetted against the bare wall of your house or garage. Its lovely lines break up the starkness of barren walls. The light grey-green foliage mass of Russian olive tucked away in the rear of your yard will add visual depth and a restful, cool oasis.

Think color, as you plan your landscapes. Reds and oranges and yellows are warm colors. Blue and green are cooler colors. You can take advantage of the cheery contrast created by masses of red petunias and white alyssum with blue lobelia against a dark-green background of Japanese yews. Yellow and white of daisies against a stately blue spruce offer a different color scheme.

If you enjoy decorating your home at Christmas, consider a spruce or fir for your lawn. They are lovely in any season, but with Christmas lights against a white ground covered with snow-laden boughs, they provide a picture for your next year's greeting cards.

Don't overlook varying greens of shrubs and trees. Some are dense and dark, others light and airy. Poplar leaves sing in the slightest breeze.

Some trees have dark, rough bark; others, gray or white. Birch trees have attractive black-and-white trunks that add contrasting interest. Some trees and bushes, too, have winter bark of gray to black, or provide yellowish to red color in an otherwise blank landscape.

The sweep of weeping willows can be wonderful. They offer light yellow in the blush of spring as they set their leaves, then flow in gorgeous green until fall turns the leaves light yellow again. However, never plant them near septic tanks or leach fields. Willows have a nasty habit of pushing roots into underground pipes to clog them shut.

As you plan, consider your outdoor living areas. Picture a white wrought-iron patio bench and table shaded by dark-green evergreens. That's an entirely different impression from a cedar picnic table bordered by a bed of red geraniums.

If you have a soggy, boggy area, don't despair—it doesn't mean a disaster. You can, of course, fill or drain the area. A more simple and rewarding approach is to develop the site with plants that prefer that type of environment. It saves time and makes good growing sense.

Some trees and shrubs actually prefer more moisture, even quite wet areas. Red or silver maples, alder, river birch, tamarack or sweet gum, swamp white oak, willow, and American arborvitea tolerate wet areas quite well.

For shrubs in damp spots, try a spice bush, Siberian dogwood, gray dogwood, hawthorn, huckleberry, winterberry, cranberry, viburnum, arrowwood, and even blueberry if the soil can be drained a bit.

Another approach makes sense, too: grow wild. Wild iris, buttercup, rose mallow, cardinal flower, asters, swamp milkweed, even various ferns can lend a natural look. Nature will do much of the work, because wild flowers are naturally

A corner planting with a taller framing tree will extend the V form of visual focus well beyond the house. Ground covers or low growing shrubs can be extended even further to the lawn tree to tie the various plantings together even more effectively.

Vary types of trees with their own unique form, shape and texture for added appeal. Here evergreen and deciduous trees with shrubs and ground covers create a naturally pleasing combination for a long, low home.

Pachysandra is one choice for a permanent ground cover in shady areas.

strong, resistant to diseases, and can tolerate conditions that cultivated plants can't. One area of every home in which we have lived has been left to its own care. We also leave a small pile of brush, a refuge for birds, rabbits, and wild creatures. The wonderful ways of nature create a new scene in this otherwise difficult-to-landscape area.

Many people enjoy their gardening activities every week. Others prefer to enjoy the look of beautifully landscaped homes, but don't relish the constant care that is involved. If you are like them, design your landscape for minimal maintenance without the bother of pruning, weeding, trimming, and other little chores each weekend.

Here are other key points to think about as you plan your plantscape. Mulch is one of the best bets. It serves a threefold purpose. Organic mulch smothers weeds and therefore saves time. It also conserves soil moisture. Third, it adds an attractive appearance around shrubs and trees, as well as slowly decomposing to provide natural nutrients in small amounts to feed your plants. You can use wood chips, ground-bark bits, peat moss, composted grass, old leaves, and leaf mold. All work well and efficiently.

Ground-cover plants have their place, too. They eliminate need for weeding and keep you from scarring tree trunks when mowing. Shaded areas beneath trees and on slopes often cause gardener's grief. Take heart. Try ground covers such as pachysandra, vinca, periwinkle, English or other ivies.

There are many others, less well known, that work well. Bearberry is a trailing evergreen with white or pink flowers in May, bright red berries in summer and fall. It's good for light, sandy soils in sun or half shade. Heath and heathers make splendid, somewhat taller carpets. They require acid, well-drained soil and some pruning. Depending on the type, they vary in stature from 6 inches to 2 feet.

Cotoneasters vary greatly in character. Low types are ideal ground covers, either creeping cotoneaster with pink flowers and bright red berries, or cranberry cotoneaster with pink flowers and showy, long-lasting, bright-red berries.

Local garden centers can guide you as well as your favorite nursery. They often have lists of available plants not on display which they can order for your landscape scheme.

To cut down on work, outline all planting beds, whether individual trees or entire hedgerows, to provide a definite demarcation between lawn and planting areas. You can use bricks sunk to soil level; strips of nonrotting wood, such as redwood, cyprus or cedar; or metal and plastic strips. Keep them right at soil level. Grass roots will stay on their side, plant and shrub roots on theirs, which reduces trimming time.

Install trees, shrubs, and flower beds in cohesive units to minimize maintenance and cut down on the amount of careful mowing and close-in work that must be done. Keep lawns free of bird baths, ponds, and other obstructions.

Consult nurserymen on tree care before you plant one that looks "so nice" in pictures. Ginkgo trees drop leaves rapidly in late summer. Crabapples and hawthorns drop fruit which can be a pick-up chore.

Ask about cultivating problems of trees and shrubs. Avoid those that require constant care unless you have the time they need.

Patios are multipurpose. You reduce the size of lawn and garden to tend, and have a play area as well. Lay a base of plastic film, add sand, then install bricks, patio blocks, or slate for a more random look. Plastic keeps weeds from germinating. Paving a patio stops the problem, too. You can plant bulbs and flowers in tubs, pots, and barrels, put them on casters, and roll color around the patio any time you like.

If you plan to do much outdoor cooking, remember that trees may not like the tangy, smoky aroma rising from your barbecue. Never build a permanent barbecue beneath a low-hanging branch. Eventually, you'll scorch the leaves and damage the limb.

Pruning is important to keep trees and shrubs looking their loveliest. If you don't care to spend time pruning properly, then pick plants that need less such care. Fruit trees, for example, let your landscape bear abundantly. But you must prune periodically to encourage new fruiting wood. You also must spray to prevent fungus diseases, rusts, and insect attacks, depending on the types of trees you raise. If that sounds like too much weekly work, avoid fruit trees.

Reducing routine landscape care should be in your basic plan. The better trees and shrubs grow without excess care, the more time you'll have to enjoy them.

As you read this chapter and others in this book, you will want to consult with local experts at nurseries and garden centers. They, of course, know local growing conditions. Also observe which plants do best in your locale, your block, and your neighborhood. You'll find a horticultural zone map and accompanying list of in-

Fallon 77

*For homes on slopes, you can achieve greater privacy with a landscaped patio
leading from a basement family room. Street noises are minimized and the plantings
also buffer noise as well as help enclose the private outdoor living room.*

dicator plants later on in this book. It's a basic guide. Some areas have frost
pockets; you may live in one. Other areas have poor soil, from shale to clay or sand.
The discussion of soil improvement in an earlier chapter can help you overcome
these problems.

As you plan, map out your landscape-look to be. Here are questions you should
keep in mind when you go shopping for the plants you want. Don't be afraid to
ask questions. Reputable nurseries and garden centers will be pleased to provide
answers. It's your money you must spend, so spend it wisely.

When you shop for plants consider these key points:

What is the mature size and shape of the plant? How will it look in relation to
your proposed planting site?

What is the color of the plant in all four seasons? Don't consider just flowers
alone, but how the plant will perform for the rest of the growing year.

Think and ask about the form of the plant in relation to other plants in your landscape, as well as structures on your property. Will big trees grow up to overpower a
ranch-style home? Conversely, will tiny trees that look nice by themselves appear
out of proportion to a tall home or building?

What is the plant's texture? A fine texture will create a feeling of space, while a
coarse texture will help enclose an area.

Ask about adaptability of the plant to your soil condition and type. Often garden
centers will do soil tests and advise what type of fertilizer may be needed to improve garden and landscaping ground.

Some plants prefer shade, others demand sun. Know your plants' needs and be certain that the area in which you will plant them suits their needs. A list of plants for sun, shade, dry, and moist conditions is included later in this book. Your local nurseryman can provide additional details. One friend became quite angry, insisting that he wanted dogwood trees, as he had had in New Jersey, for his Vermont home. Trouble was, the nurseryman wouldn't sell them because he maintained they would not be winterhardy. The homeowner finally agreed after two years of futile effort.

Look for quality plants, well branched, with no blemishes, disease, or insect damage. Low quality may be cheaper, but if they die you usually are to blame. Ask about a guarantee on quality and growth. More nurseries give one today. Look for tags with species and variety names. More plant suppliers are providing this information and cultural directions, too. Better ones include a picture of the plant with its mature characteristics, so you can judge how it will fit into your plans. Quality plants, with reasonable care from you, will give you years of landscape beauty.

After window shopping, return to your plan. Review it. Change it if necessary because of plant availability and compatibility with sun, soil, or site, and make your final shopping list.

Set time for delivery so you can move the plants to their new locations, dig in well, and get them planted right. It is always best to plant shrubs and trees the day they arrive. Next step is to dig in and get things growing well.

6.

Selecting Trees and Shrubs

Trees are the basic element in your landscape design. They set the stage on which you create your outdoor scene—around, among, and under trees. Once planted, they will last a lifetime.

Some, such as locust and pines, grow quickly. Others are slow to mature. Here is a list of good basic trees and shrubs that do well for a variety of situations. No species is superior or "best." That depends on the size, shape, and purpose you have in mind. Don't make the mistake of deciding what type you like and trying to make it grow into your plan. Consider what the tree or shrub itself needs in light, soil, growing room, and climate. From among those that will thrive in your area, select those best suited for your particular situation and desires.

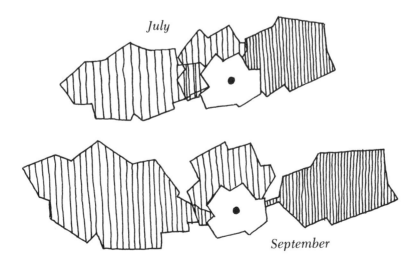

July

September

Shade pattern of 20-foot tree during summer months

Looking out, the specimen tree in your lawn is an eye-appealing sight. Looking at your home from outdoors, the shrubs and ground plantings blend the specimen tree into the total design of your home landscape.

Avoid trees that are susceptible to storm damage or hosts for common insect and disease pests. Some may drop seeds and pods, or tend to topple in sites exposed to wind and storms. Your trees are a long-term investment. Think carefully and select wisely, so they'll reward you for years to come.

Norway maple is a European native, widely planted over the Eastern United States. Nurserymen have developed special variations with darker leaves, even purplish ones. Crimson King retains its distinctive color all season. Some are columnar, which means they grow more upright than the typical spreading habit of Norway maples. These trees typically provide dense shade but have a shallow root system. It's difficult to grow grass beneath them. They can, however, tolerate city growing conditions quite well.

Red maples display their flowers early in spring. Tiny red buds burst against the smooth gray bark. These are also one of the first trees to change color in fall. Some develop brilliant red color, others have less impressive displays. Shop for fall-foliage-display trees in the fall. Among the same variety, some have more vivid coloration. They will remain true to this habit throughout their lifetime, so pick out the most brilliant when they are in full fall-color display. Red maples are easy to transplant and grow rapidly, but are somewhat susceptible to storm damage.

Sugar maples are fast growing, but their wood is brittle and limbs may be snapped by storms. They tend to clog septic fields as willows do. However, the graceful, silverish leaves and tree shape are two points in their favor.

Horse chestnuts are magnificent in spring. Long, showy flowers cover the tree like candles. It grows tall and with spreading branches, so needs lots of growing room. It produces profusions of inedible nuts, but otherwise has merits as a fine, stately shade tree. Nurserymen have double-flowered and red-flowered forms.

Ash trees, both green and white, grow rather rapidly. The green type develops a broad crown. Leaves turn bright yellow in fall, but drop rapidly. White ash becomes a larger tree. It, too, has been redeveloped by nurserymen with types that are hardier and better for home use.

American sycamores or plane trees are easily distinguished by their bark, which flakes off as the trunk expands. Some people consider it a dirty tree because of this bark-shedding habit. However, it has a big plus. This tree grows rapidly, reaches immense size, and tolerates the harsh conditions of city air pollution. The Oriental plane tree is a better bet than the native American sycamore, being less susceptible to disease.

White oaks are majestic. Their rounded outline with thick branches provides a sturdy sight in landscapes. Red oaks are faster growing. They develop a broad, round-topped look and offer deep-red fall color. These have clean growth habits and withstand city conditions well. Scarlet oaks are similar to red oaks in shape and growth habit.

Pin oaks are unique, with upper branches horizontal while lower ones droop close to the ground. You can prune away low branches and enjoy this shapely tree with its serrated leaves, or place it where it grows to full effect.

River birch has salmon-colored bark that peels off in thin layers. It does well in wet soils and offers that advantage if you have soggy areas. White birches are more graceful. The lovely bark and light, airy branching habit make this an attractive landscape tree. Birch leaf miners and borers may attack it, but these pests can be controlled with spring sprays. Multitrunked gray birches do well in clump plantings.

Lindens are among our best shade trees. They produce small flowers in spring and light-green leaves that hang on into late fall. Lindens have few insect or disease pests, which suits them for many uses. Improved varieties include a narrow, oval form, a more compact upright growth, and even pyramidal-shaped trees.

Among smaller trees, Amur maple is a roundheaded, extremely hardy tree. Its red fall color is as brilliant as any of the maples. Winged seeds hang on after leaves have fallen, for an interesting winter effect. It requires practically no attention and grows well in a wide range of soil types.

Russian olives have unique, gray-colored foliage. Flowers are inconspicuous but very fragrant. The brown, shedding bark and crooked trunk add to its picturesque look. These trees adapt to many types of soil, especially hot, dry areas.

Goldenrain tree has large, conspicuous yellow flower clusters in late June, usually after other trees have completed blooming. Bladderlike fruit follows, which look like small Chinese lanterns. The wide-spreading habit is effective in a small yard. It grows on a wide variety of soils and has few problems.

For a flowering display over the seasons, you may wish to try flowering trees: crab apples, cherries, and others.

Crab apples are splendid in bloom and they're versatile too. There are more than two hundred different types, but space permits mentioning only a few of them here. Nurseries can recommend many others.

Arnold has red buds that develop into fragrant white flowers, eventually forming small yellow to red fruit. It is densely branched and matures 12 to 15 feet tall.

Dorothea has pink and white semidouble flowers, followed by small orange-

The scene from your window, whether flowering crab apple, dogwood, or fruit trees, provides blooming beauty every spring and color in fall too.

yellow fruit. It too is densely branched, with rounded growth maturing to 20 feet.

Floribunda has pink buds, yellow to red fruit, and attains 25 to 30 feet in height.

Royalty has rosy-red flowers, small reddish-purple fruits, and purplish-red foliage during its growing season. It is upright and rounded in shape; matures at 15 feet.

Eastern redbud is another fine flowering tree. It has an irregular but attractive spreading crown with purplish pink flowers in clusters. Fall foliage is yellow. Redbud looks best in small groups or naturalized at the edge of woods. It is hardy, tolerant of many soils, and blends in nicely with other plants.

European mountain ash is regaining its old-time popularity. This upright tree spreads somewhat as it matures. It grows rapidly, with clusters of fragrant white flowers in late spring. Small orange-red berries soon form, to attract songbirds, and last until fall. The loose, compound leaves are light and airy. It may be subject to insect and disease problems, but modern sprays can control them.

Flowering cherry trees are available in many sizes and shapes. Some flowers are single, others double; white to pink to red. Cherries generally don't like wet soils. Among recommended varieties are the Kwanzan, hardiest and most reliable or oriental cherries. It has double pink flowers, upright growth, and matures about 25 feet tall.

Dogwoods have been perfected by plant breeders and nurserymen. These are among America's most popular, lovely trees, named as state trees for their beauty and performance. Typical dogwoods are rounded to upright, mature about 30 feet high, and provide spectacular white bracts with flowers before leaves form. Glossy red fruits persist into fall, and scarlet foliage adds to autumn beauty. Dogwoods in general need good soil and ample moisture to perform to perfection.

Among good varieties are Apple Blossom, with apple-pink bracts; Cherokee Chief, with red bracts and reddish leaves; and Xanthocarpa, with yellow fruit, and usually suitable for Zones 5 to 7 (see map). Northern areas are more limited in choice, and upper states usually have winters that prohibit dogwood culture for landscaping.

Oriental dogwood, with its rounded shape and horizontal branching, grows about 20 feet tall. It has large white to pink bracts, reddish-pink fruits, and scarlet fall foliage.

Flowering peach is another lovely landscape choice. Vase-shaped to spreading in growth habit, it matures about 25 feet tall. Single pink flowers appear before foliage. They do well on good soil, but require sprays to control pests that may attack fruit. Among good varieties are weeping double pink or red, with typically pendulous branches; double white, with profuse double-white flowers; late double red, with double-red blooms; and royal redleaf, with bright red foliage.

Mimosa or hardy silktree does well in southern climates. This unique tree, with its typical multiple trunks or spreading branches, matures about 30 feet. It is open and airy with delicate, fernlike leaves. Flowers are clusters of dainty pink puffs in summer.

You can grow exotic too if you wish to enjoy the rare and unusual trees. The Brooklyn Botanic Garden, Brooklyn, New York 11225, has a handbook on 1,200 trees and shrubs and where to buy them. You might consider such exotics as a

40-foot maturing Chinese chestnut that resists the chestnut blight which destroyed our American chestnut trees.

The Amur cork tree is slow growing, with massive branches and deeply furrowed, corklike bark. The Turkish filbert is a well-shaped ornamental with pyramidal habit and rough corky bark.

A goldenchain tree, with striking mid-spring, foot-long clusters of bright yellow flowers, is ornamental indeed. It is vase-shaped, grows quite rapidly, and does best in cool, moist summers.

Carolina silverbell is a moderately fast grower with delicate white, bell-shaped flowers that appear in late spring. These don't like wet or heavy soils or dry, hot areas either.

Cedar of Lebanon, false cypress, Japanese tree lilac, and Swiss tone pine add to the list of exotics that are suitable for some areas. Check your local nursery for rare specimens that suit your area, if you like the exotics.

Deciduous shrubs that drop leaves in fall also provide seasonal color and texture changes in your landscape. You may prefer them for flowers, foliage, fruit, or bark. Well-illustrated nursery catalogs provide a wide range of selections. Naturally, you will be restricted to those that tolerate the climate where you live.

Beauty bush is vigorous and upright, with an arching growth habit. In May the plant is covered with pink flowers. It grows well and requires little attention, maturing about 10 feet tall.

Crape myrtle is a large shrub in the south, maturing to about 10 feet also. Its showy flowers in late summer, ranging from white to dark red, depending on variety, are notable. It is restricted to warmer areas.

Winged euonymus is a medium-sized shrub, 8 to 10 feet tall, which functions as a specimen or can be pruned into hedges. Twigs have corky ridges. In fall, leaves turn scarlet. It roots well and needs little care. Compact varieties are available.

Lilacs are one of the joys of spring. They grow from 6 to 15 feet tall, depending on the variety. Of the hundreds of named varieties, so-called French hybrids are perhaps the most popular. They are dense, upright-growing shrubs with flowers ranging from white and pink to bluish and dark purple. Both single- and double-flowered forms are available. Proper pruning is needed to promote best flower production. After plants are established, remove one-third of the old stems each year.

Mock orange is a vigorously growing, upright shrub with white flowers in late spring, either single or double. It is grown primarily for its highly fragrant flowers. Periodic removal of old stems encourages best flowering habit each year.

Japanese maples are either a small tree or large shrub, depending on which authority you ask. With finely serrated leaves, dark-red foliage, and striking branching habit, these somewhat slow-growing trees make excellent specimens. They prefer well-drained soil, high in organic matter, and mature 10 to 20 feet tall, depending on the variety.

Rose of Sharon, at 12 feet tall, is classed as a large shrub. It bears flowers in August when few other big plants do. You may choose single or double blooms in colors from white to pink or blue. Annual pruning encourages best blooming results.

Winterberry is used primarily for its bright-red berries, which appear while leaves are still green. They remain long after leaves fall, and attract birds. Only

Children learn to appreciate nature's beauty and purpose in a well-landscaped home.

female plants produce berries, so you must be sure to plant both sexes to insure fruit production. These plants thrive in any good garden soil.

There are, of course, many other trees, deciduous and evergreen, as well as flowering trees, shrubs, and bushes for landscape designing. You can obtain free catalogs from nurseries listed at the end of this book. Local nurseries and garden centers usually have wall charts or catalog sheets, illustrating plants they can obtain for you.

Keep two points in mind. Select plants that are suited to your area and will perform in your climate. Secondly, consider the total look of your landscape scene. All plants should harmonize and blend together, rather than become a hodgepodge of specimens that don't seem to fit into the total lovely look you wish to achieve.

Tall yellow marigolds with dark foliage form a bright background for brilliant red petunias. Ageratum or similar low-growing plants in front provide a three-tiered blooming display.

7.

Pick Your Landscape Pleasure

Whether you are a beginning gardener, possessed with the urge to create a more beautiful, fulfilling outdoor environment, or a veteran gardener with years of careful cultivation behind you, the following lists can prove helpful. Often we overlook useful and valuable trees, shrubs, and flowers that could add considerably to the beauty and joy of our landscape.

More important, perhaps, these lists can guide you to achieving beauty in every season, from the time spring flowers burst forth until winter winds begin wailing. These selected lists include brief descriptions of the plants themselves. Always check with local nurseries for their adaptability to your area.

Good Flowering Shrubs

Alpine currant is a medium-size bush with greenish-yellow, fragrant, inconspicuous flowers in April. It grows in shade or sun and bears scarlet fruit.

Japanese barberry is a well-branched shrub with green foliage in summer, bronze in fall. It serves as a hedge or border. The pygmy type has red foliage in summer.

Beauty bush grows large with upright, spreading habit. Showy pink flowers in late May to June set brown seed pods. It likes full sun in borders as a specimen bush.

Cotoneaster has creeping or spreading habit with a wide selection of types. Inconspicuous pink or white flowers in dense foliage are followed by attractive red berries.

Flowering almond is a low-growing small shrub with a round top. It has double pink or white flowers in May and enjoys sunny spots.

Forsythia is available in several adaptable varieties. It traditionally blooms in early to mid-April, with upright or weeping design, depending on the type. Newer varieties have darker and more profuse yellow blooms.

Hydrangea, or snowball plant, has large white flowers. Blooms can be 6 to 10 inches across, ranging from greenish white to pinkish brown. Other varieties range from blue to pink, depending on soil acidity. By increasing soil acidity you can change pink colors to eventually blue blooms.

Lilacs scent the air in spring. Hundreds of hybrid varieties are available. They bloom best in full sun, from early to late May. Some are double, others single-flowered in graceful pyramidal spikes on tall bushes. Good for specimens or hedge effect.

Flowering quince is medium-size with reddish-pink to scarlet or coral flowers in May. Cut branches can be forced to bloom indoors, as can forsythia.

Magnolias are favorites throughout the South. Large pink, white, or purple flowers bloom in May. The saucer magnolia will become a tall tree. Other types remain somewhat smaller.

Multiflora rose is often advertised for hedges. It needs much room to roam. Quick growing, with small white flowers and red fruit for birds, it requires severe pruning to keep it in bounds. Seeds dropped by birds start this plant wandering around home grounds.

Viburnum varies in growth habit. Some are upright, useful for screens, with red fall foliage. Others have larger white flowers in May, with fruits in July and August. Check local suppliers for those best suited to your locale.

Winged euonymus, also called burning bush, has corky wings on bark. Flowers and fruits are sparse, but the fall foliage display is distinctive scarlet-pink to dark-red flame. Ideal for specimens and hedges, too. Low-growing types are suitable in mixed plantings, but do require periodic pruning.

Good Evergreen Shrubs

Japanese yews are available in upright, bushier spreading, and even smaller types. They have dark-green leaves, stand shearing well, and make fine hedges or specimens in foundation plantings.

Spreading yews may grow tall, but newer ones spread to 6 or 7 feet with rich dark-green leaves. You need pruning shears to keep them in their alloted space.

Low junipers, from Andorra to Sargent, and the ground-hugging Blue Rug are low, take full sun, and require less care in general than do yews or other junipers.

Mugho pine is a broad, round shrub with moundlike dwarf forms available for rock gardens or low border plantings. Other types grow tall and need pruning every year or so.

Pfitzer's juniper is gray-green in color. Its semispreading branches at all angles are fine on slopes and other difficult areas. Compacta is a good dwarf variety and reliable spreader.

Chinese holly makes a dense shrub, 4 to 5 feet high. It grows in shady locations. Many fine varieties, some with variegated leaves, make hollies versatile in middle and southern parts of the country.

Pyracantha, also called firethorn, grows rapidly and can be trained easily in es-palier designs. As a shrub with dark-green leaves, and bright orange-red berries in fall and winter, it deserves more attention.

Perennials provide annual beauty. Once well planted in beds, borders, as part of

Pyracantha adds its berries in late season and into early winter. You can train this attractive plant for espalier sculptures.

shrub areas, rock gardens, or where they fit your needs, perennials pop up each year to reward you again. Wise landscape specialists recommend that home owners concentrate on perennial flowers first. Once they are established, you can add annuals or change to other annuals year to year for variation.

This listing is designed to provide you with a season-to-season guide of blooming beauty for continuous color in your landscape.

Good Perennial Flowering Plants

	Plant	Color	Height (Inches)	Remarks
April	Alyssum	Yellow, gold	15	Lovely with tulips
	Anemone, pasque-flower	Purple	12	Cool location, moist soil
	Dwarf bleeding heart	Pink	18	Lacy, attractive foliage and flowers
	Dwarf iris	Purple	8	Vigorous, blooms into May and June; low-growing
	English daisy	Red, pink, white	6	Cool, moist soil; does best in partial shade
	Primrose	Violet, yellow, red	8—15	Best in cool, moist, partial shade; continues to bloom into May
May	Coral bell	Red, pink, white	18	Small flowers, excellent cut flowers from May to October
	Dwarf phlox	Pink, blue, lavender, white	6	Vigorous, covers rapidly, full sun; rock gardens
	German iris	Yellow, pink, blue, white, purple, bronze	36	May to June flowering, some again in fall
	Iceland poppy	Red, orange, pink, white	18	Delicate; will self-seed; flowers from May to October
	Oriental poppy	Orange-red	36	Vigorous, single or double flowers, foliage gone by midsummer
	Violets	Red, violet, yellow, purple, white	8	Excellent in shade; cool, moist soil
	Columbine	Blue, white, pink, purple, yellow	36	Long spurred hybrids are best and most vigorous
	Day lily	Yellow, orange, bronze, pink	12—60	Vigorous plant, some are scented; flower May to October
	Foxglove	Lavender, purple, white	24—60	Self-seeding biennial, best in partial shade

Plant	Color	Height (Inches)	Remarks
June			
Peony	Pink, white, red	30	One of the best perennials, single and double flowered; double require staking
Shasta daisy	White with yellow center	36	Large daisy flower, single and double flowers into July
Sweet William	Red, pink, white, in combinations	24	May to early July flowering, biennial, reseeds itself yearly
Siberian iris	Rose, blue, violet, white	36	Vigorous, should be divided every 3 to 4 years
July/August			
Baby's breath	White, pink	36	Fine lacy foliage and flowers through August
Beebalm	Red, pink, white	42	Scented foliage, spreads rapidly
Coreopsis	Yellow, bronze	30	Very prolific flowering plant
Delphinium	Blue, white, purple, pink	40	Tall spikes, new hybrids best
Hollyhock	White, pink, rose, maroon, red	60—100	Good background plant, double and single flowered, self-seeding biennial
Phlox	White, pink, salmon, purple	36	Large, showy, flowering into August
Black-eyed Susan	Yellow with black center	24	Rough leaves, good cut flower, nice wild touch
Cardinal flower	Red	48	Spectacular red flowers, does well in wet soils, brookside
September			
New England aster	Pink, white, violet, blue	48	Large plants with considerable variation in flower size
Plantain lily	Lavender, white	24	Large attractive leaves, grows in shade
Stonecrop	Red, white	18	Fleshy, gray-green foliage, flowers August to frost

Annual flowers can vary your outdoor color schemes from year to year.

Among the blooming beauty of annual flowers, you have a wide selection. Elsewhere you'll find a longer list, keyed to conditions they prefer, sun or shade, moist or dry. This list is designed to guide your choice of more easily grown annuals with notes about their colors, height, spread, and how they can be used outdoors or as cut flowers for indoor arrangements.

Good Annual Flowers

Plant	Color	Height (Inches)	Remarks
Ageratum	Blue or white	6—18	Pinch tips to encourage branching, remove dead flowers; part or full sun
Balsam	Reds, pinks, purples	20—30	Won't tolerate cold, wet weather; good in planters or window boxes; needs sun
Celosia, cockscomb	Reds, orange, yellow	16—40	Good for cut flowers or dried material; sun or shade
Coleus	Green and white, yellow, red, many mixtures	18—24	Grown for foliage color; good for planters or window boxes, shady areas
Cornflower	Blue, pink, red	12—36	Good for cut flowers; partial sun
Cosmos	White, pink	30—48	Good for cut flowers, background plant; needs sun
Four-o'clock	White, red	20—24	Good in formal beds, needs sun
Impatiens	White, red, orange, purple	10—20	Beautiful for flower beds in shady area, good for cut flowers
Larkspur	White, blue, purple	18—48	Difficult to transplant, buy in peat pots or cell packs; good for cut flowers; needs sun
Marigold	Orange, bronze, yellow	6—30	Good for cut flowers, window boxes and beds; needs sun
Morning glory	Blue, pink	8—12	Vine-type growth, decorative, needs sun

Plant	Color	Height (Inches)	Remarks
Nasturtium	Orange, gold, salmon	10–12	Needs well-drained, sunny soil
Pansy	Red, yellow, blue, bronze mixtures	6–10	Early spring flower, nice in rock gardens, sun or partial shade required
Petunia	Almost every color: red, pink, blue, white, bicolor	8–24	Good for window boxes, beds, blooms all summer; pick heads to force new bloom; needs sun
Phlox	Pink, white, salmon, pastels	6–12	Good in rock gardens, beds, borders; needs sun
Portulaca	Red, pink, yellow, white	6–9	Good in rock gardens in sunny area
Snapdragon	Red, yellow, bronze, white, pink	10–36	Good for cut flowers, in beds, borders, sunny area
Strawflower	Yellow, yellow with black center, red, brown, gold	30–40	Good source of cut flowers and plants for drying; needs sun
Sunflower	Yellow, dark center	48–84	Used as background, source of cut flowers, bird feed; needs sun
Sweet alyssum	White, blue	6–10	Good border plant in sunny area
Verbena	Purple, white, red, blue	9–12	Source of cut flowers, needs sun
Vinca	White, purple	15–18	Good plants for window boxes, needs sun
Zinnia	Red, rose, pink, orange, purple, cream	18–36	Source of cut flowers; beds, borders in sunny area

8.

Horticultural Zones and Guide Plants

Some plants like it hot; others prefer cooler weather. Some can withstand stark, frigid northern winters. It pays to know which plants will perform best and survive through winters where you live. Local nurseries and reputable mail-order nursery firms can guide you in selecting the best trees and shrubs for your particular area. This chapter will provide your basic guide and the facts you need to know about the ten horticultural zones in America, where they are, and which plants do best in which zones.

You should be aware that carload sales of azaleas, for example, may be tender plants grown in southern areas that just won't thrive in northern climates with cold winters. You may also prefer some trees, like dogwoods, which you enjoyed in a previous home. However, they may not prefer the climate of your new area.

All plants, of course, have special needs for sun, water, and nutrients. Some like shade, others prefer full sunlight. Local nursery experts can guide you on individual plant requirements so you can place them where they will thrive, in the right conditions they prefer, around your home grounds.

Happily, The National Arboretum of the U.S. Department of Agriculture, in cooperation with the American Horticultural Society, has developed excellent plant indicator guidelines. These so-called Indicator Plant Examples serve as a handy reference to typical plants that can thrive in the various horticultural zones.

The Superintendent of Documents in Washington, D.C., offers a colorful horticultural zone map, which includes details of tree and shrub groups that thrive in the respective zones. Both map and list are graded by the lowest average annual temperatures in each zone. Local plant suppliers can add to the list, based on their experience in your particular area.

Even in some zones, there are local variations. You'll notice that spring comes several weeks earlier just a few miles away. Large bodies of water, from lakes to rivers, modify climates. That's why grapes grow so well along the Finger Lakes of New York and azaleas blaze beautifully along the Carolina coast. Here's the Indicator Plant Example list for ready reference as you plan your own landscape.

Indicator Plant Examples

Zone Number	Common Name	Botanical Name
Zone 1 (below −50° F.)	Dwarf birch Crowberry Quaking aspen Pennsylvania cinquefoil Lapland rhododendron Netleaf willow	*Betula glandulosa* *Empetrum nigrum* *Populus tremuloides* *Potentilla pennsylvanica* *Rhododendron lapponicum* *Salix reticulata*
Zone 2 (−50° to −40° F.)	Paper birch Bunchberry dogwood Silverberry Eastern larch Bush cinquefoil American cranberry bush	*Betula papyrifera* *Cornus canadensis* *Elaeagnus commutata* *Larix laricina* *Potentilla fruticosa* *Viburnum trilobum*
Zone 3 (−40° to −30° F.)	Japanese barberry Russian olive Common juniper Tatarian honeysuckle Siberian crab apple American arborvitae	*Berberis thunbergii* *Elaeagnus angustifolia* *Juniperus communis* *Lonicera tatarica* *Malus baccata* *Thuja occidentalis*
Zone 4 (−30° to −20° F.)	Sugar maple Panicle hydrangea Chinese juniper Amur River privet Virginia creeper Vanhoutte spirea	*Acer saccharum* *Hydrangea paniculata* *Juniperus chinensis* *Ligustrum amurense* *Parthenocissus quinquefolia* *Spiraea vanhouttei*
Zone 5 (−20° to −10° F.)	Flowering dogwood Slender deutzia Common privet Boston ivy Japanese rose Japanese yew	*Cornus florida* *Deutzia gracilis* *Ligustrum vulgare* *Parthenocissus tricuspidata* *Rosa multiflora* *Taxus cuspidata*
Zone 6 (−10° to 0° F.)	Japanese maple Common box Winter creeper English ivy American holly California privet	*Acer palmatum* *Buxus sempervirens* *Euonymus fortunei* *Hedera helix* *Ilex opaca* *Ligustrum ovalifolium*
Zone 7 (0° to 10° F.)	Bigleaf maple Kurume azaleas Atlas cedar Small-leaf contoneaster English holly English yew	*Acer macrophyllum* *Azalea Kurume* hybrids *Cedrus atlantica* *Contoneaster microphylla* *Ilex aquifolium* *Taxus baccata*

Indicator Plant Examples

Zone Number	Common Name	Botanical Name
Zone 8 (10° to 20° F.)		
	Strawberry tree	*Arbutus unedo*
	Mexican orange	*Choisya ternata*
	New Zealand daisy bush	*Olearia haastii*
	Japanese pittosporum	*Pittosporum tobira*
	Cherry laurel	*Prunus laurocerasus*
	Laurestinus	*Viburnum tinus*
Zone 9 (20° to 30° F.)		
	Asparagus fern	*Asparagus plumosus*
	Tasmanian blue gum	*Eucalyptus globulus*
	Bush cherry	*Eugenia paniculata*
	Fuchsia	*Fuchsia* hybrids
	Silk oak	*Grevillea robusta*
	California pepper tree	*Schinus molle*
Zone 10 (30° to 40° F.)		
	Bougainvillea	*Bougainvillea spectabilis*
	Golden shower	*Cassia fistula*
	Lemon eucalyptus	*Eucalyptus citriodora*
	Rubber plant	*Ficus elastica*
	Banana	*Musa ensete*
	Royal palm	*Roystonea regia*

The map in this chapter details the expected minimum temperatures in most of the important continental areas of the United States. With predicted trends of colder winters over the next few years, there may be variations downward.

However, the cold-hardiness zones of the map are based on isotherms of average minimum winter temperatures for the years from 1899 to 1938. Adjustments are made for thirty-four states on the basis of January mean minimum temperatures for 1931 through 1952, from records of the U.S. Weather Bureau.

Information from other sources has been modified or reinterpreted in many local areas to conform with recent and more detailed data from state experiment stations and individual cooperators in this long-range project. Extensive data has been the foundation of these zones.

The map is a guide. The indicator plants are based on proven facts as they apply to each zone. Other factors should be considered too, of course. You must realize that temperatures of adjacent zones do become similar near their common boundary. There also are colder or milder climates within the zones. There may be islands in hilly or mountain areas and variations in warmer valleys between mountains. In developing this total map, weather-station reports from sites in valleys where temperatures tend to be somewhat milder and where plants are normally grown have been used.

Rainfall, humidity, soil characteristics, duration and intensity of sunlight, all influence plant growth in each zone, too.

The map zones and indicator plant lists have been most useful in determining minimum temperature survival of plants in the specific areas. After all, you can im-

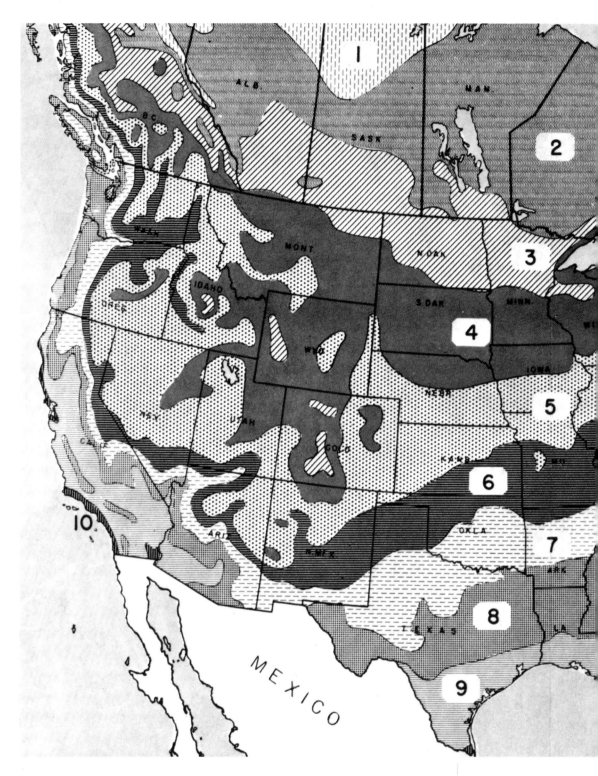

prove soil, fertilize, water, and tend plants, but you can do little about the weather and the winter conditions that ultimately affect plant survival.

Naturally, a plant that thrives in one part of a given zone is likely to do well in other parts of the same zone or warmer ones. Remember, as you choose your trees and shrubs, that the zone in which a given plant may survive is not necessarily the zone in which it will do best. Remember, too, that a plant or several plants may die in a particularly harsh winter because of poor care, or from other factors.

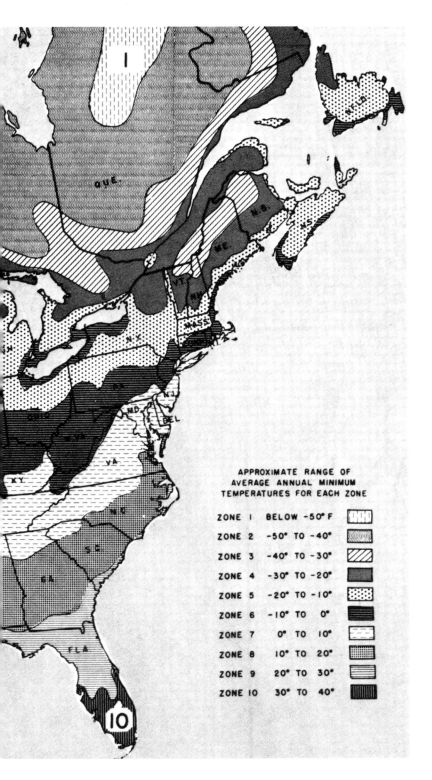

APPROXIMATE RANGE OF
AVERAGE ANNUAL MINIMUM
TEMPERATURES FOR EACH ZONE

ZONE 1   BELOW -50° F
ZONE 2   -50° TO -40°
ZONE 3   -40° TO -30°
ZONE 4   -30° TO -20°
ZONE 5   -20° TO -10°
ZONE 6   -10° TO   0°
ZONE 7   0° TO 10°
ZONE 8   10° TO 20°
ZONE 9   20° TO 30°
ZONE 10 30° TO 40°

Since so many families and individuals move to new homes in new areas each year, it helps to have available and understand this basic horticultural zone information. It is a reliable guide, as are the indicator plant lists.

Once you pick your plants and put them in place, it's up to you to provide the necessary care, food and water, and protection from insects and diseases that will enable your plants to become a permanent part of your lovelier landscape, for years to come.

Berries are a treat and add to gardening fun from a fruitful landscape planting.

9.

Enjoy Fruitful Landscapes

You can enjoy tastier living from your own backyard. Fact is, dwarf fruit trees bear well on porch or patio, too. You can plant a strawberry barrel, a blueberry bush in a patio pot, or dwarf peach trees in a redwood barrel. Today, with fruit prices astronomical, adding multipurpose berry bushes and fruit trees to home landscapes is fun, delicious, and economical.

Fortunately, nursery experts and plant breeders have used their talents well. Dwarf fruit trees are blooming fun. They add spring color with gorgeous displays, then reward you again with delicious, full-size fruit. Dwarf trees are produced by grafting desired tasty varieties on special rootstocks. This keeps the trees smaller. They bear earlier, take less space, and are much easier to tend than full-size trees. And they serve well as decorative accents in your home landscape. You can grow dwarf peach, pear, cherry, or apple trees of all types in a small backyard plot. We do. In one border, only 8 feet wide by 100 feet long, we enjoy Northern Spy, Red and Yellow Delicious, McIntosh, and Lodi apples. We also have dwarf Bartlett and Clapps Favorite pears, Bing cherries, and both peaches and nectarines from bountifully bearing dwarf fruit trees.

You can enjoy toothsome treats of blueberries, blackberries, and raspberries, among the bush fruits. All do quite well in most parts of the country. Once planted, they propagate themselves by shoots and runners underground to form thick hedges. That makes the bramble-type berry bushes ideal for property border hedges, as screens for separating garden areas, or in their own established beds. Tilling deeply is important to let these perennial berry favorites grow a strong roothold. In a year or two they fill in well. Most bush fruits begin yielding their second year. With proper pruning, they will continue year after year to yield their delicious harvests.

Strawberries can be grown in beds and borders too. You might try a pyramid planting or a strawberry barrel. To stretch your harvest season, choose everbearing varieties. They yield in spring, some in summer, then another big crop in fall.

Many local garden centers and nurseries offer berries. Old established mail-order nurseries like Starks, Bountiful Ridge, Sterns, and Burpee, among others, have colorful, informative catalogs to help you make the right selections.

Dwarf fruit trees enjoy the same growing conditions that standard-size trees do. They should be planted where they receive full sun, in fertile soil. Because they have smaller root balls and growing habits, you can easily improve the soil which will be their home. Mix in peat and compost and manure if available. Use one part peat, one part compost, one part manure to three parts soil. You can vary that formula if your soil is especially sandy or too full of clay. Peat and compost help open heavy-clay soils. They also, happily, help improve the water-holding capacity of sandy soils that tend to dry out.

Dig your hole large enough to allow bare-rooted trees to spread roots naturally. Fill the hole half full of soil and water well. If you buy balled and burlapped or container-grown trees, remove the binding or container and carefully place the soil ball around the roots in the hole. Then fill half full with soil. Tamp it down and water well.

Tamping and watering help eliminate large air pockets. Then add the remaining, improved soil mixture and water well again. Leave a saucer-shaped depression around newly planted trees. That helps catch rain to keep soil moist as trees begin to set new root hairs and feeding roots. Mulch around new trees to retain soil moisture and smother weeds. Stake or support the trees the first year until they gain a firm and sturdy roothold.

Pruning is quite easy. In my book *Landscape You Can Eat* or others on fruit trees and berries, you'll find details of pruning and pest control. Some folks avoid fruit trees because they worry about attacks from hoards of harmful insect pests. With today's much safer, easy-to-use pesticides, you can banish bugs and reap the bountiful, fruitful harvests you deserve. A simple hose-end sprayer is all it takes, because dwarf trees don't grow too tall. Dwarf peaches may mature 6 to 8 feet high at most. Dwarf pears and apples reach 15 or so feet high. That also makes picking easier.

Berry bushes belong in every home landscape. Black, red, and purple raspberries are costly in stores. A small patch can yield dozens of quarts year after year.

Berries fit in almost anywhere, because they can thrive even in less-than-perfect growing or soil conditions.

Raspberries and blackberries can be planted as canes. Select a full sunny location. Early spring is the best planting time. Prepare soil deeply and well for these permanent parts of your fruitful landscape. The more organic material you dig or till into soil, the better the plants will perform.

Soak bare-rooted plants in water. Mix a slurry of compost humus or well-rotted manure, one part per ten parts water. Let roots soak in this an hour or so. It softens roots and gets them ready for their new home.

Set raspberries and blackberries 2 feet apart. If you plant rows, space them 6 to 8 feet apart. New shoots will fill in the gaps within the rows, but you need room for care and harvest between rows.

Slit the soil with a spade blade. Insert roots and fluff them out. Then cover, tamp soil down well, and water. Red raspberries and blackberries should be set a few inches deeper than in the original nursery. Place container-grown stock with the root ball even with the soil surface. Plant black and purple raspberries the same depth as in the nursery. You can spot the soil line on the canes, just above the areas of root formation.

Blueberries and blueberry pie go together well. You can grow blueberries in your garden if you provide the more acid, moist, but well-drained soil conditions they prefer. Blueberries are shallow-rooted. Newer home-garden varieties yield huge, succulent berries in abundance from attractive shrubs. These flower nicely in spring, produce their fruit, then provide lovely foliage displays in fall. You can improve acid conditions by avoiding use of lime around the plantings and mulching well year after year with oak leaves, pine needles, and ground pine bark, just as you should for rhododendrons, which like more acid soil.

New blueberry varieties from the plant breeders are bushier, lower growing, and heavier yielding. That makes many ideal for container cultivation. Pick a large redwood patio planter, 18 inches deep and 18 to 24 inches in diameter. You may also use large clay pots or more decorative tubs. Place an inch or so of gravel in the bottom to provide good drainage. Mix one part loamy soil with one part peat moss, one part humus, and one part sand. Fill the container half full, spread out the plant roots, and fill to just below the top.

Water well until the plant takes hold. Then water weekly, especially at fruiting time, so berries are as plump and juicy as you wish.

Outdoors, plant blueberries in a group, along a walk as fruitful shrubs, or in your garden. Remember, they need acid soil and other plants like sweeter growing conditions. Usually, blueberries should be by themselves or grouped near rhododendrons and azaleas. Plants with similar growing needs should always be together. They'll like it better and reward you more prolifically when they're happy.

Strawberries are one of America's favorite fruits. They also are versatile. You have an advantage in your garden. Sweeter, tastier varieties can be grown in the garden, in pots or tubs, or in strawberry barrels. These tastier varieties may not suit commercial growers because they don't ship well and yield abundantly at one time. That's great for you because you can enjoy the better flavor, picked right from the plants, and have them many more weeks if you plant the everbearing kind.

With all fruit trees, berry bushes, and plants, keep in mind that some yield early, others in mid-season, and some bear late, right up to fall frost. It pays to check your garden catalogs to become familiar with the bearing habits of different varieties. That way, you can select and grow the ones that give you flavorful eating through the seasons, from spring to fall.

There's a secret to planting strawberries properly. They should be planted with their crowns right at the soil level. The drawing in this chapter shows you how. You can grow them in beds or rows. They also provide flowers as border displays before producing their colorful, red, ripe, juicy fruits.

A strawberry tub or barrel is a welcome addition to an apartment balcony or patio. You can buy wood or large clay containers with holes spaced around them. Fill the planter to the first layer with good soil mixed with compost or prepared houseplant potting soil. Insert roots through the holes, cover with soil, and fill to the next level. Repeat the process until the job is done. Then add flowers or more strawberry plants on top. Place the tub on a caster base to roll it where you wish.

Dwarf fruit trees and berry-bearing plants can help you enjoy tastier living from your more fruitful landscape.

Masses of similar color are more effective than mixtures of many colors in landscape design.

10.

Flowers for Every Purpose

Whether you plan beds or borders, aspire to window boxes of blooming beauty, or wish to make shady spots sparkle, there are flowers for every location and purpose. Some prefer full sun, others like shade. Some are known for their fragrant perfume. Others are noted for their ability to thrive, even in poor or dry soil. Some are best in moist areas.

The list that follows gives you a wide choice of sizes, colors, and blooming ability for every place you want to plantscape with annuals and perennials. You'll find the best flowers for cutting or rock gardens, hanging baskets or edging. Many of these flowers are available in seed racks each spring at garden centers and local stores. You may also wish to order from reputable mail-order firms. You will also find, at the end of this book, the names and addresses of mail-order nurseries and plant firms. They offer free catalogs that fully describe flowers and vegetables, as well as trees, vines, and shrubs for your landscape needs. Thanks to the W. Atlee Burpee people for their help in compiling this detailed list.

Plants for Partial Shade

Ageratum
Anchusa
Astilbe
Azalea
Begonia
Bleeding heart
Boston ivy
Caladium
Coleus
Columbine
Coral bells
Ferns
Forget-me-not
Foxglove
Impatiens

Lily of the valley
Lobelia
Mock orange
Nemophila
Nicotiana
Pachysandra
Pansy
Periwinkle
Plumbago
Polyanthus
Sweet violet
Torenia
Vinca
Viola

Bright tulips against a stone wall welcome spring in glorious display. An espalier shrub adds its natural lines to the stone wall.

86

Perennials from Seed

Achillea
Alyssum
Anchusa
Anemone
Anthemis
Arabis
Aster
Aubrietia
Campanula
Candytuft
Carnation
Centaurea
Cerastium
Cheiranthus
Chinese lantern
Chrysanthemum
Columbine
Coreopsis
Delphinium
Dianthus
Forget-me-not
Gaillardia
Geum
Gloriosa daisies
Gypsophila

Helianthemum
Hemerocallis
Heuchera
Hibiscus
Hollyhock
Iberis
Lathyrus Latifolius
Lavender
Lilies
Linum
Lupine
Lychnis
Nepeta
Penstemon
Polyanthus
Poppy
Pyrethrum
Rudbeckia
Scabiosa
Shasta daisy
Statice
Tritoma
Verbena venosa
Viola

Tall Flowers for Backgrounds

Canna
Celosia—tall
Cleome
Cosmos
Dahlia—tall
Delphinium
Foxglove
Gladiolus
Gloriosa daisies

Hibiscus
Hollyhock
Marigold—tall
Nicotiana
Snapdragon—tall
Sunflower
Sweet sultan
Tithonia
Zinnia—tall

Looking for Fragrance?

Alyssum
Carnation
Clematis paniculata
Heliotrope
Lavender
Lilacs
Lilies
Lily of the valley
Mignonette
Mock orange
Nicotiana

Peony
Petunia
Phlox
Rose
Stock
Sweet pea
Sweetshrub
Sweet sultan
Tuberose
Wallflower
Wisteria

Dwarf Plants for Edging

Ageratum
Alyssum
Aster—dwarf
Begonia
Celosia—dwarf
English daisy

Lobelia
Marigold—dwarf
Pansy
Portulaca
Viola
Zinnia—dwarf

Window Box

Alyssum
Asparagus Sprengeri
Begonia
Celosia—dwarf
Coleus
Geranium

Ivy
Lobelia
Marigold—dwarf
Petunia
Verbena
Vinca

For Dry or Poor Soils

Achillea
Alyssum
Brachycome
Bridal wreath
Cactus
California poppy
Calliopsis
Candytuft
Celosia
Centaurea montana
Cleome
Coreopsis
Cosmos
Dianthus
Euphorbia
Four-o'clocks
Gaillardia
Gloriosa daisies
Godetia

Gypsophila
Helianthemum
Honeysuckle
Iris
Lathyrus latifolius
Linum
Lupine
Lychnis
Marigold
Mugho pine
Nasturtium
Petunia
Phlox
Poppy
Portulaca
Potentilla (Gold Drop)
Verbena
Vicia

Plants for Bedding

Aster
Balsam
Begonia
Dahlia
Geranium
Impatiens
Iris
Marigold
Nicotiana

Pansy
Petunia
Portulaca
Salvia
Snapdragon
Verbena
Vinca rosea
Viola
Zinnia

Fall crocus bear bright blooms as brown leaves begin to fall.

For Hanging Baskets

Asparagus fern	Nasturtium
Begonia	Petunia
Lobelia	Thunbergia

Best Flowers for Cutting

Achillea	Gloriosa daisies
Anchusa	Gypsophila
Anthemis	Heuchera
Arctotis	Iris
Aster	Larkspur
Bells of Ireland	Lathyrus
Calendula	Marigold
Carnation	Nigella
Celosia	Pansy
Chrysanthemum	Peony
Columbine	Petunia
Coreopsis	Poppy
Cornflower	Pyrethrum
Cosmos	Rose
Cynoglossum	Scabiosa
Dahlia	Shasta daisy
Delphinium	Snapdragon
Dianthus	Stock
"Everlasting" flowers	Sweet pea
Forget-me-not	Sweet sultan
Foxglove	Sweet William
Gaillardia	Verbena
Gerbera	Viola
Geum	Wallflower
Gladiolus	Zinnia

Easiest-to-Grow Annuals

Alyssum	Marigold
Anchusa	Mignonette
Aster	Nasturtium
Balsam	Nigella
Calendula	Night-scented stock
California poppy	Phlox
Candytuft	Poppy
Celosia	Portulaca
Cornflower	Scabiosa
Cosmos	Strawflower
Gaillardia	Sunflower
Godetia	Sweet pea
Larkspur	Zinnia
Linaria	

Plants for Moist Places

Astilbe
Caladium
Ferns
Forget-me-not
Foxglove
Impatiens
Lily of the valley
Nicotiana
Polyanthus
Sweet violet
Vinca
Viola

For Rock Gardens

Ageratum
Alyssum
Arabis
Aubrietia
Brachycome
California poppy
Candytuft
Cerastium
Dianthus
Dimorphotheca
Forget-me-not
Gazania
Helianthemum
Heuchera
Juniper—Andorra
Linaria
Lobelia
Marigold—dwarf
Nemophila
Nierembergia
Phlox
Portulaca
Verbena
Zinnia—dwarf

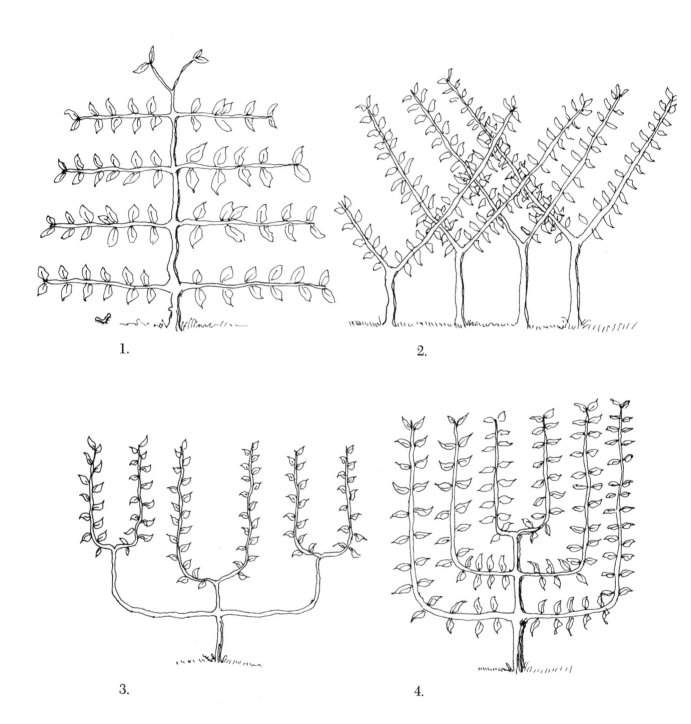

Espalier designs add a distinctive touch to home landscapes. These are examples of 1. Horizontal T, 2. Belgian Fence, 3. Triple U-Shaped Upright Cordon, 4. Palmette Verrier.

11.

Enjoy Espalier Decor

You can become a sculptor or a sculptress in your own home grounds. All you need is a sharp pair of pruning shears. It's really quite easy to create dramatic and distinctive living sculptures with trees, shrubs, and vines. The technique is ages old. You can revive this ancient art to produce eye-catching displays wherever you live. Even potted plants can be trained to appealing shapes far different than they would have by growing normally.

Espalier culture was practiced by the ancient Romans. Exotically shaped trees and vines graced their villas and formed lovely vistas around their homes. Today, you can recapture that living art form to make plants perform for you in wondrous ways. Many trees and shrubs have a natural tendency to follow unique growing patterns. With a little help from you and your well-sharpened pruning shears, they'll perform in striking and spectacular ways.

The word *espalier* is a French word. It means shoulder or support. The English borrowed the word in the seventeenth century to describe the growth patterns achieved by training trees, vines, and shrubs to trellises or frames. This living-sculpture training of plants gained fame throughout Europe long ago. It still thrives there in many formal gardens.

Today, there is renewed interest in this age-old way of creating distinctively different shapes of plants as outdoor accents in home plantscapes. It does require some knowledge and attention to careful pruning techniques. Once you learn the secrets, described in this chapter, you too can imaginatively create a wide range of living sculptures year by year.

The secret of satisfying results with espalier is to begin with a young tree or shrub, whether already in your home grounds or available from a local nursery. Pick one with several well-balanced limbs off the main trunk. As a guide, the best varieties suited for city or suburb, sun or shade, are listed at the end of this chapter, with both common and Latin names. The simplest pattern is a fan or hand. You can grow much more exotic if you wish.

Often you find plants well branched near the ground. These are easily trained to flatten against a background. Such plants can completely and dramatically change a barren wall.

The background against which you train your espalier determines the type of support you must provide. You can use trellises of wood, wires attached to frame buildings, or a fence. Steel reinforcing rods used in construction are inexpensive. They can be bent to determined shapes, cemented in the ground, and your plant's branches secured to them as you train your tree.

Place rods or other supports at least 6 inches from a building so leaves can grow properly. Air movement between wall and plant is important, too, both for ease of painting and maintaining your building and to avoid building damage from the plant's constant rubbing against a wall.

Tie selected limbs to the supports with short lengths of soft twine or plastic-coated or weather-resistant plastic rope. Uncoated wire will soon cut into bark, damaging branches and providing easy access for insects and disease to penetrate and attack the plant.

Fasten the cord securely enough to hold the branch in its intended position. Don't tie it too tight or it may girdle the branch. Check ties periodically to be certain none is cutting into branches. Loosen those that seem too tight. Take up the slack on others to force branches into your desired pattern or design.

If you are training larger limbs, run plastic-coated wire through old lengths of garden hose. This prevents wire from chafing the bark or biting into it if winds cause constant movement.

You can secure and support espaliers against brick or stone walls in several ways. The best is with lead-headed nails, available from garden centers or hardware stores. Drive these into the mortar. Then bend the lead tongue attached to the head over to secure each branch. Loop ties of coated wire, attached to concrete nails, or anchored eye screws also work well.

Old clothesline can be dyed or painted for use in training espalier trees and shrubs. Use green or some other natural color so the ties blend unobtrusively into the background.

Proper staking and tying are important. The key to success in creating dramatic designs, however, is careful pruning. In this chapter you will find illustrations of several living sculpture patterns. Almost any design can be worked out with proper pruning and necessary training. You can pursue a branched candelabra or checkerboard pattern. Cordon effects work well against wide wall expanses. The simpler the design, the easier it is to maintain. Fancier designs require extra effort, but are certainly much more dramatically eye-catching.

The first step in space sculpturing begins with pencil and paper. Sketch the wall, building area, chimney, or whatever area you wish to plantscape. Then read through the list of suggested specimens in this chapter that lend themselves naturally to espalier culture. Pick out a pattern that pleases you.

Pyracantha is a popular and easily trained plant for espalier. It offers blooms in spring and its bright berries last long into every fall. Dwarf fruit trees are natural choices, too. They add a fruitful touch for eye and taste appeal.

After planting, secure selected limbs or branches that will be the main scaffolds of your desired espalier design. Then prune away all undesired branches. Anytime stray branchlets appear, prune them off close to the main stem or scaffold branches. Remove shoots that distract from your desired pattern.

Prune deciduous espaliers when flower buds form, so you can preserve the blooms and berries where you want them. If side or lateral shoots appear to conflict with your design, remove them back to the main stem. Whenever tender new branchlets grow in an undesired direction, pinch the tips off. This encourages bushier growth in the direction you want. The plant's strength also is focused in the direction you want your design to take its sculptured shape.

Pruning, of course, encourages new growth to form. Since regularly pruned espalier plants do tend to sprout new growth continuously, root pruning may be necessary too.

Dig a shallow trench about two feet from the trunk of the tree or vine. For smaller plants, root-prune by spading around the low-growing espalier plants. This prevents overly lush growth and new sprouts that emerge to detract from your original design.

Simplest rule of all: save your sketch. Every month or so, look at your budding espalier designs. If they are growing excessively or out of style and shape, take pruning shears in hand and remove all unwanted branches, shoots, and excess growth.

Some plants respond easily and quickly. Others take a year or two before they shape up to your desires. Prune and tie and prune again. Plants are indeed like people. They too can be trained to perform in more beautiful and acceptable ways when you know how and have the patience to train them properly.

Your choice of plants for espalier training is virtually unlimited. You can select from an extremely large variety of trees, shrubs, and vines. Some are evergreen; others are deciduous. You must, of course, consider the individual plant's hardiness, its adaptability to soil types, plus the location you can provide and the maintenance required. There are other factors, too, from the plant's adaptability to training to its growth rate and need for more frequent or severe pruning. Foliage habit, texture, and ornamental effects of bark, flowers, and fruit all play a role in your decision, naturally.

To help with that decision, here's a brief list. There are more plants that could be used, of course. However, for starters these trees and shrubs are suitable. This list is divided into sections based on need for sun or shade, use in city or suburbia. They also are separated by flowering characteristics, foliage or fruit effect, and their growth habit that fits them best for single or multistory buildings.

Spring-Flowering

Flowering quince—*Chaenomeles speciosa*
Forsythia—*Forsythia* species
Oriental cherry and cultivars—*Prunus serrulata*
Weeping higan cherry—*Prunus subhirtella* 'Pendula'

Summer-Flowering

Japanese dogwood—*Cornus kousa*
Mock orange—*Philadelphus* species
Korean stewartia—*Stewartia koreana*
Five-stamen tamarix—*Tamarix pentandra*
Viburnum—*Viburnum sieboldii*

Summer Foliage Displays

Japanese maple and cultivars—*Acer palmatum*
Spreading cotoneaster—*Cotoneaster divaricata*
Willow-leaved cotoneaster—*Cotoneaster salicifolia* 'Floccosa'
Japanese holly and cultivars—*Ilex crenata*
Chinese juniper and cultivars—*Juniperus chinensis*
Andorra juniper—*Juniperus horizontalis* 'Plumosa'
Japanese white pine—*Pinus parviflora* 'Glauca'
Japanese snowball—*Viburnum plicatum*

Autumn Foliage Displays

Japanese maple and cultivars—*Acer palmatum*
Japanese dogwood—*Cornus kousa*
Spreading cotoneaster—*Cotoneaster divaricata*
Winged euonymus—*Euonymus alatus*
Oriental cherry and cultivars—*Prunus serrulata*
Korean stewartia—*Stewartia koreana*

Fine for One-Story Buildings

Japanese maple—*Acer palmatum*
White redbud—*Cercis canadensis* 'Alba'
Spreading cotoneaster—*Cotoneaster divaricata*
Rock cotoneaster—*Cotoneaster horizontalis*
Japanese holly and cultivars—*Ilex crenata*
Juniper—*Juniperus* species
Star magnolia—*Magnolia stellata*
Bristlecone pine—*Pinus aristata*
Firethorn—*Pyracantha coccinea* 'Lalandei'
Yew—*Taxus* species
Viburnum—*Viburnum* species

Fine for Multistory Buildings

Blue atlas cedar—*Cedrus atlantica* 'Glauca'
Redbud—*Cercis canadensis*
Japanese dogwood—*Cornus kousa*
Cornelian cherry—*Cornus mas*
Forsythia—*Forsythia* species
Japanese holly and cultivars—*Ilex crenata*
Water goldenchain—*Laburnum watereri*
Crab apple—*Malus* species
Japanese white pine—*Pinus parviflora* 'Glauca'
Oriental cherry and cultivars—*Prunus serrulata*
Yew—*Taxus* species
Viburnum—*Viburnum* species

Species for Shade

Flowering quince—*Chaenomeles speciosa*
Winged euonymus—*Euonymus alatus*
Japanese holly and cultivars—*Ilex crenata*
Water goldenchain—*Laburnum watereri*
Firethorn—*Pyracantha coccinea* 'Lalandei'
Dwarf Japanese yew—*Taxus cuspidata* 'Nana'
Japanese snowball—*Viburnum plicatum*

Best Decorative Trees for Espalier

Japanese maple—*Acer palmatum*
Flowering dogwood—*Cornus florida*
Japanese dogwood—*Cornus kousa*
Cornelian cherry—*Cornus mas*
American holly—*Ilex opaca*
Juniper—*Juniperus* species
Goldenchain—*Laburnum* species
Crab apple—*Malus* species
Pine—*Pinus* species
Oriental cherry and cultivars—*Prunus serrulata*
Weeping higan cherry—*Prunus subhirtella* 'Pendula'
Stewartia—*Stewartia* species

Best Vines for Espalier

Bittersweet—*Celastrus* species
Wintercreeper and cultivars—*Euonymus fortunei*
Climbing hydrangea—*Hydrangea anomala petiolaris*
Climbers and dwarf shrubs—*Rosa* species
Japanese wisteria—*Wisteria floribunda*

Good in Containers

Japanese maple and cultivars—*Acer palmatum*
Sargent juniper—*Juniperus chinensis 'Sargentii'*
Water goldenchain—*Laburnum watereri*
Star magnolia—*Magnolia stellata*
Dorothea crabapple—*Malus 'Dorothea'*
Red jade crabapple—*Malus 'Red Jade'*
Oriental cherry and cultivars—*Prunus serrulata*
Weeping higan cherry—*Prunus subhirtella 'Pendula'*
Firethorn—*Pyracantha coccinea 'Lalandei'*

Good for City Gardens

Chinese redbud—*Cercis chinensis*
Winged euonymus—*Euonymus alatus*
Forsythia—*Forsythia* species
Japanese holly and cultivars—*Ilex crenata*
Bristlecone pine—*Pinus aristata*
Japanese white pine—*Pinus parviflora 'Glauca'*
Yew—*Taxus* species
Japanese snowball—*Viburnum plicatum*

Fruitful Accents

Spreading cotoneaster—*Cotoneaster divaricata*
Franchet cotoneaster—*Cotoneaster franchetii*
Rock cotoneaster—*Cotoneaster horizontalis*
Dorothea crab apple—*Malus 'Dorothea'*
Red jade crab apple—*Malus 'Red Jade'*
Hardy orange—*Poncirus trifoliata*
Firethorn—*Pyracantha coccinea 'Lalandei'*
Yew—*Taxus* species
Viburnum—*Viburnum* species

Species for Sun

White redbud—*Cercis canadensis 'Alba'*
Flowering quince—*Chaenomeles speciosa*
Japanese dogwood—*Cornus kousa*
Rock cotoneaster—*Cotoneaster horizontalis*
Winged euonymus—*Euonymus alatus*
Forsythia—*Forsythia* species
Saucer magnolia—*Magnolia soulangiana*
Star magnolia—*Magnolia stellata*
Red jade crab apple—*Malus 'Red Jade'*
Yew—*Taxus* species
Siebold viburnum—*Viburnum sieboldii*

12.

America's State Trees and Flowers

If you have uprooted yourself from your native soil and moved to what you hoped would be greener pastures, your new landscape may look different. Buck up.

Every state has its state tree and flower, familiar to every native son and daughter. Most of these plants can be transplanted to your own personal new habitat. You must, of course, determine whether the climate and winterhardiness of the plants will mesh with the conditions in your new area.

In some cases, official actions by state legislatures have named the state tree, flower, or both. In other cases, the plant is unofficially the state tree or flower by generally public use.

This chapter lists state trees and flowers. Horticultural magazines list nurseries that specialize in wild or native plants.

State Trees

Alabama—"Southern pine": Slash pine *(Pinus caribaea)*; Longleaf pine *(P. palustris)*; and Loblolly pine *(P. taeda)*

Alaska—Sitka spruce *(Picea sitchensis)*

Arizona—Arizona cypress *(Cupressus arizonica)*

Arkansas—"Pine"

California—Redwood *(Sequoia sempervirens)*

Colorado—Colorado blue spruce *(Picea pungens 'Glauca')*

Connecticut—White oak *(Quercus alba)*

Delaware—American holly *(Ilex opaca)*

District of Columbia—Scarlet oak *(Quercus coccinea)*

Florida—Cabbage palmetto *(Sabal palmetto)*

Georgia—Live oak *(Quercus virginiana)*

Hawaii—Kuki or candlenut *(Aleurites moluccana)*

Idaho—Western white pine *(Pinus monticola)*

Illinois—"Native oak"

Indiana—Tulip tree, tulip, or yellow poplar *(Liriodendron tulipifera)*

Iowa—"Oak" *(Quercus* species)

Kansas—Cottonwood *(Populus deltoides* or *balsamifera)*

Kentucky—Tulip tree, tulip, or yellow poplar *(Liriodendron tulipifera)*

Louisiana—Southern magnolia *(Magnolia grandiflora)*

Maine—White pine *(Pinus strobus)*

Maryland—White oak *(Quercus alba)*

Massachusetts—American elm *(Ulmus americana)*

Michigan—"Apple"

Minnesota—White pine *(Pinus strobus)*

Mississippi—Southern magnolia *(Magnolia grandiflora)*

Missouri—Flowering dogwood *(Cornus florida)*

Montana—Western yellow pine *(Pinus ponderosa)*

Nebraska—American elm *(Ulmus americana)*

Nevada—Trembling aspen *(Populus tremuloides)*

New Hampshire—Canoe birch *(Betula papyrifera)*

New Jersey—Red oak *(Quercus borealis)*

New Mexico—Pinon or nut pine *(Pinus edulis)*

New York—Sugar maple *(Acer saccharum)*

North Carolina—Tulip tree, tulip, or yellow poplar *(Liriodendron tulipifera)*

North Dakota—Green ash *(Fraxinus pennsylvanica lanceolata)*

Ohio—Ohio buckeye *(Aesculus glabra)*

Oklahoma—Redbud *(Cercis canadensis)*

Oregon—Douglas fir *(Pseudotsuga menziesii)*

Pennsylvania—Canada hemlock *(Tsuga canadensis)*

Rhode Island—Sugar maple *(Acer saccharum)*

South Carolina—Cabbage palmetto *(Sabal palmetto)*

South Dakota—Cottonwood *(Populus deltoides* or *balsamifera)*

Tennessee—Tulip tree or tulip poplar *(Liriodendron tulipifera)*

Texas—Pecan *(Carya pecan)*

Utah—Colorado blue spruce *(Picea pungens 'Glauca')*

Vermont—Sugar maple *(Acer saccharum)*

Virginia—Flowering dogwood *(Cornus florida)*

Washington—Western hemlock *(Tsuga heterophylla)*

West Virginia—Sugar maple *(Acer saccharum)*
Wisconsin—Sugar maple *(Acer saccharum)*
Wyoming—Cottonwood *(Populus deltoides* or *balsamifera)*

State Flowers

Alabama—Camellia
Alaska—Forget-me-not
Arizona—Saguaro cactus
Arkansas—Apple blossom
California—Golden poppy
Colorado—Columbine
Connecticut—Mountain laurel
Delaware—Peach blossom
District of Columbia—American Beauty rose
Florida—Orange blossom
Georgia—Cherokee rose
Hawaii—Hibiscus
Idaho—Syringa
Illinois—Violet
Indiana—Peony
Iowa—Wild rose
Kansas—Wild sunflower
Kentucky—Goldenrod
Louisiana—Magnolia
Maine—Pinecone and, tassel
Maryland—Black-eyed Susan
Massachusetts—Mayflower
Michigan—Apple blossom
Minnesota—Lady's slipper
Mississippi—Magnolia
Missouri—Hawthorn
Montana—Bitterroot
Nebraska—Goldenrod
Nevada—Sagebrush
New Hampshire—Purple lilac
New Jersey—Violet
New Mexico—Yucca
New York—Rose
North Carolina—Dogwood
North Dakota—Wild rose

Ohio—Scarlet carnation
Oklahoma—Mistletoe
Oregon—Oregon grape
Pennsylvania—Mountain laurel
Rhode Island—Violet
South Carolina—Yellow jasmine
South Dakota—American pasqueflower
Tennessee—Iris
Texas—Bluebonnet
Utah—Sego lily
Vermont—Red clover
Virginia—Dogwood
Washington—Rhododendron
West Virginia—Rhododendron
Wisconsin—Violet
Wyoming—Indian paintbrush

Observe proper planting methods as you would for all trees, shrubs, and flowers. Mail-order nurseries also provide planting and culture instructions with the plants they sell. They'll guide you to the right sun, soil, and site conditions that will enable these native specimens to sprout, grow, and thrive.

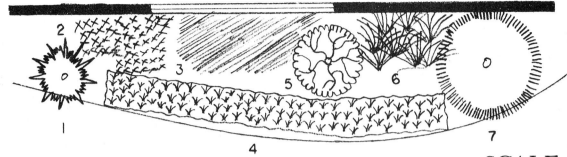

Plant List —*Sunny Window*

	Botanical Name	*Common Name*
1.	*Juniperus sargentii*	Sargent's juniper
2.	*Iris germanica*	German iris
3.	*Pachysandra terminalis*	Japanese spurge, pachysandra
4.	*Liriope sp.*	Liriope
5.	*Paeonia*	Peony
6.	*Hemerocallis*	Day lily
7.	*Taxus cuspidata capitata*	Pyramid yew

SCALE: 1'' = 3'0''

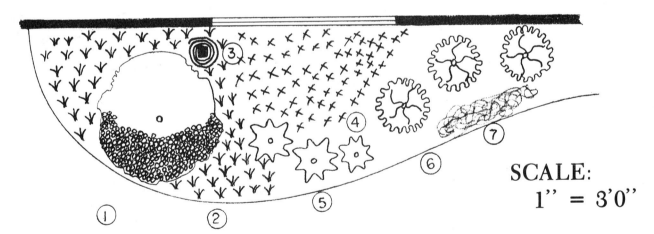

Plant List —*Shady Window*

	Botanical Name	*Common Name*
1.	*Kalmia latifolia*	Mountain laurel
2.	*Convallaria majalis*	Lily of the valley
3.	*Clematis*	Clematis
4.	*Caladium bicolor*	Caladiums
5.	*Hosta sp.*	Hosta lily
6.	*Hypericum*	Hypericum
7.	*Sedum acre*	Moss sedum

SCALE: 1'' = 3'0''

13.

Windows, Patios, and Slopes

Window View Beauty

Windows are for looking out, and to let the sunshine into your home. Many people design their outdoor landscapes with an eye to the appealing view as guests approach their home. Yet we all spend much time indoors, especially looking out from a window in the kitchen or family room. That view, too, should be planned for the most pleasing perspective possible.

Look out the windows of the rooms you use most frequently. Think how you can improve the view from where you sit or work. Here are two simple plans to gain a lovelier view.

If you live in northern areas, plan to include some evergreens to provide foliage in winter months. If you can see the garden from indoors without being close to the window, consider color coordination of the outdoor flowers with your indoor color scheme.

Here's a basic, easy-to-create, sunny picture-window planting. Focal point is a double-flowered peony. Tall bearded iris flank the other side of the window. You can use tulips for spring color, followed by annuals in the same area. Day lilies add late summer color. Depending on the total look you wish to achieve to complement your house style and shape, you can flank windows with upright or spreading evergreens. Mugho pine on one side and a tall Hick's yew on the other side of your window can bracket the color of flowers below the window. In southern areas, you might select flowering shrubs instead of evergreens. An alternate might be fruitful ones.

If you have a shady window, you can still create a look of loveliness and blooming beauty too. Select shade-loving plants that will thrive and actually prefer to be somewhat shielded from excess bright sunlight.

If your window is near a house corner which usually requires a taller shrub planting to soften stark lines, you might select shade-tolerant flowering shrubs. This window-garden design uses low-growing plants beneath the window that flow into the more striking taller specimens.

A rhododendron or azalea can provide dramatic effect. Hosta or columbine and tuberous begonias, caladium, or coleus can be planted below the window itself. They can be flanked by low-growing evergreens. Lily of the valley perfumes the air, and prefers shaded conditions.

You may be tempted to frame a window with symmetrical plantings. If you really prefer that, fine. However, a symmetrical planting tends to call more attention to the window itself than may be desired from an architectural point of view. Professional landscape architects and horticulturalists suggest the more unstructured, informal design.

Plan a Patio Party

As you develop your outdoor living environment, plan for two patio parties. The first one will help you install it. The second is your thank-you for those friendly neighbors who helped you put it all together.

Bricks in sand are an easy on the eye, attractive, durable, and pleasant outdoor paving. They are easy to install, too. Bricks are small, lightweight, and add their naturally mellow color and texture to your living plants. Flagstones also add a nice touch. Here's how to put your pleasant patio living area together.

Choose hard-burned brick for paving. Soft bricks may crack. Slick-faced new or cleaned old brick also work well. Order enough bricks to do the entire job at one time so they will match. Lots of bricks may vary in color and in texture. You can complete sections over several weekends as time permits.

You can lay bricks with open or closed joints. Where no mortar is used, closed joints are best, with bricks butted tightly together. Herringbone or basketweave are popular patterns, but more difficult to lay than the usual running-bond pattern.

For a 100-square-foot patio, a good size for family fun, you'll need these material and tools:

> 500 bricks
> 1 ton of ¼-inch crushed rock
> 5 cubic feet of coarse sand
> 2" x 4" or 2" x 6" redwood lumber
> 1" x 2" x 12" stakes
> Round-point shovel
> Flat-point spade
> Hammer (heavy)
> Level
> Iron tamp or heavy post
> Brick set
> Broom

The lumber is for edging. The amount you need will depend on the shape used and closeness of structures such as home or wall where edging may not be necessary. Use redwood, cedar, or cypress, which don't rot.

Here are four fine designs for creating your outdoor living patio with bricks or flagstones. You can make patios and paths in random patterns or more formal designs if you prefer.

Measure the size of the patio area. Order all your materials. Walks should be at least 4 feet wide. A small patio may be less work to build, but consider one of 500 square feet. It gives you ample room for most family functions, from just sitting to backyard neighborhood barbecue parties.

Grade the area to be paved. Dig out existing soil or fill 6 to 8 inches deep The paving of gravel (as the underlayer), sand, and brick will require a depth of about 6 inches. Use a 2 x 4-inch board to level the grade after digging. Place a carpenter's level on the board to slope the patio away from the house for proper drainage. It should drop in grade about 1 inch in each 8 feet.

Install the redwood lumber to edge the patio. Secure it in place with wood stakes. To thwart weeds, lay black plastic sheets on the soil surface before adding the gravel layer. The gravel holds it in place and weeds won't pop up to disturb your patio surface.

Now add a 3- to 4-inch layer of crushed stone and level it. Tamp it down firmly. Next, spread ½ inch of coarse sand over the stone and level it, using your 2 x 4-inch board. Next, set bricks on the sand. Place them slightly higher than desired as they will settle. It is best to begin in the center, just as you would when laying a tile floor indoors. Work to the outside. By careful measurement, you can end up with whole bricks wherever possible.

As you place bricks, tamp them firmly as they are set. Place a board over the bricks and use a hammer to set the bricks in the sand base. Lay all bricks that do not need cutting. Then cut those necessary this easy way:

Place the brick on a stout board. Place a brick set, a brick-cutting device, on the brick at the point where you wish to cut. Strike the set sharply with a heavy hammer. A few tests will give you the feel for doing this neatly and precisely.

After all bricks are in place, cover the paved surface with sand. Sweep it into the cracks, and your patio will be ready for use after you remove the redwood edging.

To add to your outdoor pleasure, visit a flea market, garage sale, or your garden center. Look for eye-catching decorative planters, tubs, large old pots. These can provide portable patio color every season of your outdoor living year.

Always add a layer of gravel to the bottom of the pots to insure proper drainage. Use good topsoil. Better yet, mix equal parts of soil, peat moss, and composted humus. Then plant bulbs, flowers, even strawberries if you wish. Put a caster base beneath your planter and you can roll it merrily about whenever you wish.

Planting Tips for a Steep Slope

Houses on slopes let you live a multistoried life. Basement family and game rooms open out to patios of privacy, shielded from road-level noises.

You can, of course, build tiers and terraces, or design a complete rock garden on the slope with sun- or shade-loving plants, depending on conditions. Junipers and other spreading plants also can provide solutions to fairly steep slopes. This design lets you have more color and variety in your landscape.

For lawn areas, use erosion nets or burlap strips to hold soil in place while seed sprouts and takes root. After that, grass usually checks erosion problems.

At each corner, multitrunk birch trees can be utilized to break up corners. Beneath these medium-size trees, ground covers can be planted. For more attractive

Pots, tubs, and hanging baskets all can be used effectively to provide portable color around patio, porch, or home garden.

appearance, low-growing shrubs are better. They also increase your privacy. An espalier tree or vine can be used on the basement wall behind a flower-bed or rock-garden planting.

For a multipurpose fruitful landscape in keeping with your multilevel living, add a dwarf apple and a pear or two. They mature only 10 to 15 feet tall and are accessible for care and picking. Add a patio tub or two if you wish. On casters, they can be rolled out of the way when you wish to barbecue or party. You may elect to edge your patio with dwarf marigolds, petunias, or other low-growing annuals. Strawberries mixed with marigolds are tasteful. Brackets can be attached to the walls near patio basement doors for hanging plants. Just move them inside your family room before fall frosts.

A long, low house needs trees and shrubs of various sizes and shapes to break up its stark, long lines. Here a deciduous tree provides shade to windows. Beneath it, ground cover and bedding flowers add color and greenery. Rounded evergreens frame the door, letting their trim lines round out the upright porch lines.

A pine at the side of the garage hides the barren wall, and with its airy evergreen foliage, adds a visually pleasing dimension to the lawn.

Attractive lawns also add value to your home. Much has already been written elsewhere about building and maintaining lovely lawns. Several key points should be emphasized here. Quality seed is a wise investment. It costs more, but considering the labor of building the lawn and tending it, good seed produces much more satisfying results.

Feed lawns spring and fall. Strong, healthy, well-nourished lawns help choke out undesirable weeds. Use a weed-and-feed fertilizer as necessary to eliminate the nasty broad-leaved weeds that may crop up. Realtors point out that a neatly trimmed, weed-free lawn adds immeasurably to a home's resale value. Buyers seem to feel that a home with a tidy, attractive lawn also has been well cared for itself. That adds up to increased dollar value when you wish to sell your house.

14.

Sources

Gardening is growing better every year. Unfortunately, many garden centers often stock a somewhat limited choice of shrubs and trees. Local nurseries usually have a wider selection of landscape plants. If you have some favorite plants that aren't available locally, here is a list of reputable, long-established plant firms. They offer free catalogs, packed with beautiful color illustrations that let you see how a tree, shrub, or flowering plant will appear. As you plan your home plantscaping, it helps to visualize the scenes you wish to grow. These catalogs also have valuable information about plant hardiness, shape of plants at maturity, and growing habits. Use them with this book as you plan and plant.

Bountiful Ridge Nursery
Princess Anne, Maryland 21853

Burgess Seed and Plant Company
Box 2000
Galesburg, Mississippi 49053

W. Atlee Burpee Company
300 Park Avenue
Warminster, Pennsylvania 18974

Comstock, Ferre, and Company
Wethersfield, Connecticut 06109

Farmer Seed and Nursery
Faribault, Minnesota 55021

Henry Field Seed and Nursery
407 Sycamore Street
Shenandoah, Iowa 51601

Gurney Seed and Nursery
1448 Page Street
Yankton, South Dakota 57078

Earl May Seed and Nursery
6032 Elm Street
Shenandoah, Iowa 51601

Nichols Garden Nursery
1190 North Pacific Highway
Albany, Oregon 97321

Geo. W. Park Seed Company
Greenwood, South Carolina 29646

Stark Brothers
Louisiana, Missouri 63353

Index